330.1
D347
AF685402

STUDIES IN HISTORY, ECONOMICS AND PUBLIC LAW

Edited by the

FACULTY OF POLITICAL SCIENCE
OF COLUMBIA UNIVERSITY

NUMBER 534

STUDIES IN THE THEORY OF WELFARE ECONOMICS

BY

MELVIN WARREN REDER

STUDIES IN THE THEORY OF WELFARE ECONOMICS

BY

MELVIN WARREN REDER, Ph.D.

Assistant Professor of Economics
Carnegie Institute of Technology

NEW YORK

COLUMBIA UNIVERSITY PRESS

1947

COPYRIGHT, 1947

BY

COLUMBIA UNIVERSITY PRESS

PRINTED IN THE UNITED STATES OF AMERICA

HOPE COLLEGE LIBRARY

31444

Published in Great Britain and India

by

GEOFFREY CUMBERLEGE

OXFORD UNIVERSITY PRESS

London and Bombay

To
C.P.R.

PREFACE

In this book, we attempt to explore some of the implications of welfare theory as it has been developed in the last few years. The first four chapters contain a rather brief review of this development. They have no pretension of originality; should the reader find anything in these chapters that he believes to be new, he may take it as prima facie evidence either of missing some of the literature or of finding a mistake. However, it is necessary to provide this review because so much of the literature is scattered throughout the technical journals. Professor Lerner's excellent " Economics of Control " contains much of this material, but unfortunately he does not make explicit use of the " Compensation Principle," and as this principle is central to our treatment of the subject it is not always possible merely to refer the reader to the relevant section of Professor Lerner's book. Chapters V through VIII contain what we believe to be some new developments in the theory of welfare economics on the " static " level.

Part II consists of a rather extensive sketch of a theory of dynamic economics. Chapter IX is, in one sense, not at all new. The treatments of Samuelson and Lange contain, in nuce, virtually the whole of this chapter. However, their work is highly mathematical and extremely condensed and therefore, we dare to hope that we have, in spelling it out and putting it in verbal form, made some contribution to the field. Chapters X through XII contain what are intended as original extensions of the theory expounded in Chapter IX. Chapter XIII applies this theory to welfare problems, and thus lays the groundwork for a dynamic theory of welfare economics. With the exception of Chapter XIII, this whole section is in the nature of a rather extensive, although (we hope) useful digression.

In Part III we analyze the concept of " full employment " in the light of the welfare criterion. In doing so, we have not altogether avoided the temptation to digress in order to comment on the appropriate measures for achieving it. However, for the most part we have restrained ourselves and have not written a book on fiscal policy.

The reader may often feel that we leave a problem just as we get to the heart of it, or even before. This is likely to be particularly true in connection with Part III. However justified this complaint may be, we should like to remind the reader of our intentions: we are not attempting to write a book on any of the various subjects on which we touch. We wish only to show their welfare implications; and hence we have been compelled to treat many topics from a special point of view, leaving many of their most important facets unexamined.

My greatest intellectual debt is to Professor Oscar Lange whose teaching and encouragement have been a major source of inspiration to me over a period of years; the first draft of this manuscript benefited greatly by his criticism. Professor J. M. Clark graciously suffered through two drafts of this book and made many helpful suggestions. Professors A. F. Burns, Abraham Wald, and Harold Hotelling all read parts of the manuscript and offered valuable criticisms. The book also benefited from Professor Norman Buchanan's sagacious comments on both style and content. I am also deeply grateful to Professor F. C. Mills, who was an unfailing source of advice and encouragement throughout the long process of putting ideas on paper. Mr. W. S. Vickrey has read the galleys with much care and made many helpful suggestions and corrections which materially improved the final product.

Last but not least, my wife who typed both drafts of the manuscript and in addition suffered through many a tedious evening while I labored in the throes of composition, deserves more than the usual thanks and condolences. It is to her that this book is dedicated.

As usual, the author wishes to absolve any and all parties other than himself from any errors or shortcomings that may be discovered.

October 15, 1946
Pittsburgh, Pa.

TABLE OF CONTENTS

PART I

THE STATIC THEORY OF WELFARE ECONOMICS

CHAPTER I

THE WELFARE CONCEPT

I. Definition

WELFARE economics is the branch of economic science that attempts to establish and apply criteria of propriety to economic policies. It is apparent on reflection that "welfare" has been intimately associated with "positive" economics from the inception of economic thinking. Indeed, until the latter part of the nineteenth century there was no distinction made between welfare and positive economics. Economic treatises combined advocacy with analysis in a quite uncritical manner; and very often the analysis was made subservient to the policies advocated. However, the growth and improvement of scientific standards in the economics profession has made it necessary to establish explicitly the criteria by which economists declare policies economically sound or unsound.

Much of welfare economics merely makes explicit the criteria which were implicit in the works of the classical economists, e.g. Smith, Ricardo, Mill et al.; the criteria by which they declared free trade "good", state monopolies "bad" etc. But in making these criteria explicit, many vulgar and dogmatic prejudices, masquerading as the "truths" of economics, have been exposed—and the consequent re-analysis has placed the findings of the science on a much sounder basis. Old dogmas of economic policy, presumably true for all times, places and conditions, have been shown to be valid only under certain special circumstances. No longer can economics be said to be a mere rationalization of laissez-faire. Laissez-faire can be shown to be the appropriate economic policy under, and only under, certain very definite conditions. Other policies are more advisable, economically, for other circumstances.

At one point in the evolution of economic thought, it was felt that welfare economics was unscientific; that it was normative and was hence a branch of Ethics and that, in any case, it had no place in Economics. This view, which seems to be of diminishing importance, would appear to be based on an unduly narrow view of the nature of science. Welfare economics is scientific in exactly the same sense that Medicine is. To be sure, Medicine tends to be normative; its objective, implicitly and explicitly, is to maintain " good health ", defined by optimal body temperature, blood pressure, pulse, etc. The study of organic processes which constitutes Medical Science is, however, quite independent of this objective. It is conceivable that we might try to keep temperatures at 102 degrees fahrenheit, and use all our medical knowledge to that end; the present objective of medicine is only one of a large number of conceivable objectives. Similarly, welfare economics is normative; but given its norm, the determination of the policies to be undertaken in accordance with it is a strictly scientific enterprise.

The norm which welfare economists customarily adopt is that the welfare of the community as a whole should be maximized. This is unambiguous once welfare is adequately defined. But welfare has been defined in many diverse ways and the appropriateness of economic policies will vary, depending upon the definition adopted.

The definition which we adopt has had considerable currency in the recent theoretical literature on the subject,[1] and has become almost " the " standard definition. Instead of attempting to give " content " to the idea of welfare directly, we define a welfare indicator which increases and decreases with welfare—welfare is that which varies with this indicator. The indicator is defined as follows: *welfare increases (decreases) whenever one or more individuals become more (less) satisfied*[2]

1 See the writings of Hicks, Hotelling, Kaldor, Lange, Lerner, Scitovzsky, *et al.* Detailed references to this literature are given throughout Part I.

2 An individual is said to become more (less) satisfied if he is put onto a higher (lower) indifference surface.

without any other individuals becoming less (more) satisfied. Thus the welfare of the community is said to be a maximum if its productive resources are utilized in such a way that it is impossible to make any one person more satisfied (put on a higher indifference surface) without making at least one other person less satisfied (put on a lower indifference surface). Every person in the community is included, but this is merely the result of the preferences of economists who have the ethical norms of modern Western Culture. It would be equally possible to develop a theory of welfare economics for Nazi Germany, in which only the well-being of Aryans was included, etc.[3] However, we shall confine ourselves to the usual broad scope of the welfare concept and, unless otherwise stated, we shall be thinking of maximizing the welfare of a community with a closed economy.[4]

As we have defined it, welfare[5] can be increased only when (at least) one person is made more satisfied without making anyone else less satisfied. However, there are very few eco-

3 Professor J. R. Hicks ("The Foundations of Welfare Economics," *Economic Journal*, Dec., 1939, pp. 699-700) argues that it is unscientific for the investigator arbitrarily to set up his own criteria of what is good for society, and then to judge the economic efficiency of a system in terms of these arbitrary goals. We must disagree with Prof. Hicks on this point. The nature of the objective cannot be scientific or otherwise; science is concerned only with the method by which we determine whether or not (or to what extent) the criterion adopted is satisfied. One can be perfectly scientific in determining whether an economic system conduces to the consumption of the vegetarian's ideal diet even though one may feel that such an objective is both arbitrary and absurd.

4 Usually economists have in mind a closed economy unless they are explicitly dealing with international trade. But when welfare problems of international trade are discussed, economists often present two sets of findings; one from the world's point of view and one from that of the individual nation. The policy recommendations often vary with the point of view adopted. *Cf.* T. de Scitovzsky, "A Reconsideration of the Theory of Tariffs," *Review of Economic Studies*, pp. 89-110, Summer 1942.

5 This definition of welfare was first advanced in a clear form by Harold Hotelling, "The General Welfare in Relationship to Problems of Taxes and Railway and Utility Rates," *Econometrica*, July, 1938, pp. 242-269.

nomic policies that do not involve injury to someone, even if only indirectly, and if our welfare criterion were applicable only to the few policies that harm no one, welfare economics would be quite sterile. Fortunately, this is not the case.

To show this, let us introduce the concept of a compensating tax (bounty). A tax (bounty) levied upon (paid to) a given individual is said to be "compensating" if the amount of money taken from (paid to) him in the event of an economic reorganization [6] leaves him on the (same) indifference surface he would have been on had the reorganization not occurred; i.e. a compensating tax (bounty) (a bounty is a negative tax) cancels ("compensates" for) the effect of a reorganization, leaving the individual on the (same) indifference surface he would have been on, had no changes in the situation occurred —hence the term "compensating".[7]

With the aid of this concept, we can ascertain how any given economic reorganization will affect the welfare of the community. Thus: *an economic reorganization will increase, de-*

6 We shall say that, if the amount of any product (factor) produced (used) by any firm or consumed (used directly) by any individual varies from one period of time to another there has been an economic reorganization.

7 A compensating tax may be any kind of tax whatever, so long as it has the definitive characteristics. It is perhaps most simple to think of it as a flat levy on each individual in question that is independent of any current or future economic activity he undertakes.

There is a certain ambiguity in the definition of the compensating tax (bounty) which has drawn rather extensive comment, particularly from Professor Hicks (*Cf.* J. R. Hicks' "Consumers' Surplus and Index Numbers," *Review of Economic Studies*, Summer, 1942, pp. 126-37.) The ambiguity results from the following fact: if an individual is in one position on his preference surface, A, and a reorganization moves him to another position, B, the compensating tax (bounty) necessary to restore him to the indifference surface on which A is located will, in general, differ from that necessary to perform the analogous operation if he were to be shifted from the position, B, to the position, A. The relative differences in the compensating taxes (bounties) will approach zero as a limit as B approaches A. This ambiguity becomes significant whenever an attempt is made to measure the compensating tax or bounty. In such cases, it is necessary to specify not only the shift in consumption pattern, but also the starting point. However, for most problems covered in this book, this ambiguity is unimportant.

crease or leave welfare unaffected according to whether the algebraic sum of the compensating taxes and bounties (levied on all affected persons) is postive, negative or zero. This means that if the state could collect enough revenue from those who benefited by a reorganization (without making any of them worse off than they would have been had the reorganization not occurred) to compensate fully those harmed by the reorganization (leave them as well off as they would have been in the absence of the reorganization) and retain a surplus, it could, by distributing the surplus, increase welfare.

We shall designate this property of the welfare concept by the name "Compensation Principle." Briefly, the following proposition is referred to as the Compensation Principle: *Welfare will be increased, decreased or left unchanged by a given economic reorganization depending upon whether the algebraic sum of all compensating taxes and bounties is positive, negative or zero.*[8]

2. Assumptions and Limitations of the Welfare Concept

The critical reader will perceive that there is a certain ambiguity in the preceding discussion. For, on our definition, welfare will be increased only if someone (at least) *is* made more satisfied without making anyone less satisfied, while the Compensation Principle requires only that there should be some policy of taxation that *could* lead to an increase in welfare. A given reorganization might satisfy the Compensation Principle without increasing welfare; that is, the reorganization coupled with the application of the Compensation Principle, would increase welfare; but without the application of this principle, it would merely benefit some persons at the expense of others.

If some persons are made more satisfied, but others less, by

8 This statement is that currently accepted in the literature on this subject. However, it does not consider the effects of actually paying (or not paying) compensation to those injured by a reorganization. On this point, see below, Chapter VIII.

a given reorganization, then that reorganization cannot be judged by the welfare criterion, as we have defined it. It might be that *if* the Compensation principle *were* applied, the given reorganization would (or would not) increase welfare; but it does not follow that without Compensation the reorganization will (or will not) increase welfare.

It would be possible to judge the welfare effect of reorganizations that increased the satisfaction of some individuals, while decreasing that of others, only if we had some way of comparing the satisfaction of one person with that of another. Older work on the subject, such as that of Pigou,[9] implicitly assumed the inter-personal comparability of satisfactions and hence was not restricted in this way. However, the trenchant criticism of Professor Robbins [10] and others has made economists wary of the epistemological pitfalls involved in making such assumptions and in almost all recent work on welfare problems it has not been assumed that satisfactions are comparable inter-personally.[11]

Epistemological criticism of the utility concept has not stopped with an attack on the validity of inter-personal comparisons of satisfactions, but has gone on to deny that utility is a quantifiable concept and to assert that utility cannot be represented by cardinal, but only by ordinal numbers. The definition of utility as a cardinal number involves the specification of "utility units" (this is the *sine qua non* of a marginal utility curve). On the other hand, an "ordinal definition" merely requires that we be able to state that a given individual either prefers one combination of commodities, A, to another combination, B, or prefers B to A, or that he is indifferent between the two;

9 A. C. Pigou, *The Economics of Welfare*, Macmillan Company, 4th edition, 1932.

10 Lionel Robbins, *The Nature and Significance of Economic Science*, Macmillan Co., 2nd edition, 1935, pp. 136-43.

11 A notable exception is A. P. Lerner, *The Economics of Control*, Macmillan, 1944, Chapter III. Professor Lerner's argument fails to convince me, but it is deserving of careful consideration.

that preferences be transitive, i.e. if combination A is preferred to combination B and B is preferred to C, then A is preferred to C; and that the scale of preferences be definite; i.e. no two indifference surfaces have a common point.

The cardinal definition implies all that the ordinal definition does and more. The " more " that it implies may be stated as follows: if we substitute for a utility function, $U = \phi(X_1, X_2 \cdots X_n)$ the arbitrary function, $U = \psi(X_1, X_2 \cdots X_n)$ such that $\psi_{X_i}' > 0$ whenever $\phi_{X_i}' > 0$ (where $i = 1, 2 \cdots n$) we must be able to determine whether ϕ or ψ is the individual's utility function and to do this we must be able to measure utility. So far as the author is aware, there has never been proposed a satisfactory method for determining whether the individual's utility function was ϕ or ψ.[12] Consequently many economists (including the present writer) feel that the cardinal definition of utility as usually stated, is meaningless and is, at best, useless for our purpose.[13] In any case, we can construct a theory of welfare economics without assuming the measurability of utility; but every statement we shall make would be true even if utility could be measured. If the reader feels

12 However, attempts have been made to " measure " the marginal utility of money. For example, Irving Fisher, *Mathematical Investigations in the Theory of Value and Prices*, New Haven, 1892; and *A Statistical Method for Measuring " Marginal Utility " and Testing the Justice of a Progressive Income Tax*, Economic Essays Contributed in Honor of John Bates Clark, edited by Jacob H. Hollander, New York, Macmillan, 1927, pp. 157-193. Also Ragnar Frisch, *New Methods of Measuring Marginal Utility*, Tubingen, 1932.

13 To be more specific, the author feels that in order for a definition of a quantity to be acceptable, it must state operationally the units in which the quantity is measured. That is, it must be possible to specify the actual operations whose performance constitutes a measurement of the quantity in question; e. g. we must state how we could show that an individual received (say) only one unit of utility from an extra unit of a given commodity (assuming given quantities of all other commodities) and not two or one and a half. In the author's opinion the utility concept as usually defined does not meet this test.

Von Neumann and Morgenstern, *Theory of Games and Economic Behavior*, Princeton University Press, 1944, pp. 15-31, show that under certain con-

that utility is measurable he is free to develop the theory further on his own account.[14]

Our refusal to attempt inter-personal comparisons of utility makes it impossible to judge, on welfare grounds, the propriety of measures involving (or aiming at) a redistribution of income or wealth. Many readers may feel that this conception of welfare unduly limits the scope of welfare economics. It cannot be denied that the range of problems with which this kind of welfare economics deals is very limited when compared with the broad sweep of social phenomena encompassed by the welfare economics of writers such as Hobson and Hawtrey (or even the somewhat narrower work of Pigou). But intellectual self-restraint is the price of freedom from epistemological qualms. If bolder spirits wish to venture farther afield they may, but at least they can accompany us as far as we go.

It may also be felt that on those problems which it does tackle, welfare economics does not shed sufficient light to justify the painstaking analyses that its technique requires. One of the objectives of this book is to show just what basis there is for such a view. However, it is well to remember that even the negative conclusions, with which we must often be contented, are by no means valueless, as they may serve to deflate wide-spread misconceptions that have been fostered by previous economic analysis.

---

ditions, utility is measurable. However, as they admit, it is (on their definition) impossible to compare utilities inter-personally and therefore there is no great advantage for our purpose in treating utility as a measurable concept.

14 Professor Oscar Lange has indicated a possible line of development involving the direct evaluation of the importance of the various members of the community. *Cf.* O. Lange, "The Foundations of Welfare Economics," *Econometrica,* July–October, 1942, pp. 215-28, especially pp. 219-24.

CHAPTER II

THE MARGINAL CONDITIONS OF MAXIMUM WELFARE

In the first five sections of this chapter, we shall set out the first order conditions for attaining maximum welfare which have been baptized, by Hicks,[1] the *marginal* conditions of maximum welfare. These conditions are by no means new and have been set out in detail in the works of Hicks, Lerner and Lange;[2] our discussion of them is merely a brief review of their treatments and readers conversant with this literature may find it convenient to skim through or even skip this chapter.

In our analysis of the marginal conditions of maximum welfare we shall make the following customary assumptions: 1. that each individual has one utility function (including his preferences between work and leisure) and owns definite quantities (which may be zero) of each product and each factor; and 2. that each firm has a given transformation function determined by the "state of the arts."

The marginal conditions of maximum welfare are all deduced directly from the definition of maximum welfare: maximum welfare is achieved when it is impossible to make one person better off without making some other person worse off. The first of these conditions we shall call

1. The Optimum[3] Allocation of Products

Products will *not* be allocated in the optimal manner so long as it is possible for any pair of individuals to exchange any

1 J. R. Hicks, *op. cit.*

2 J. R. Hicks, *op. cit.*; O. Lange, *op. cit.*; A. P. Lerner, *op. cit.*, especially Chapters VI and IX.

3 We shall hereafter refer (for brevity) to welfare-maximizing arrangements as optimum arrangements.

quantity of any pair of consumer goods with an increase of satisfaction to one and (at least) no loss (of satisfaction) to the other. This implies that an optimum allocation of products will be one such that no exchanges of this kind are possible. In fact, this is the definitive characteristic of an optimum allocation of products.

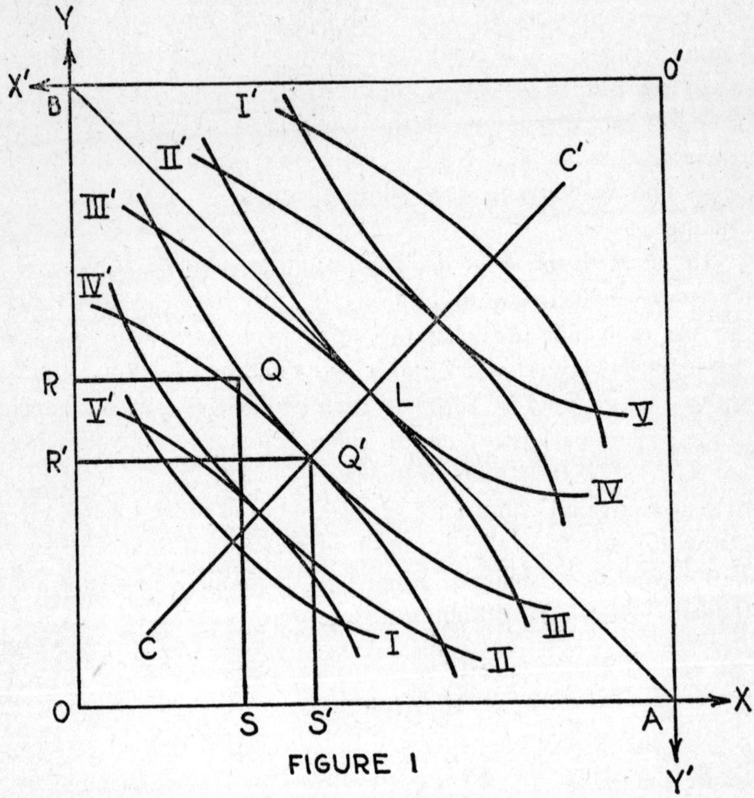

FIGURE 1

To show the implications of an optimum allocation of consumer goods, we have constructed figure 1. On its X and Y axes are measured the quantities of any two products, X and Y, purchased (consumed) by individual 1 and on axes X′ and Y′ which are inverted, the analogous quantities for individual 2.

Let us assume that the total quantities of X and Y available to the pair of individuals 1 and 2 are OA and OB, respectively; the quantities of all other products consumed by both individuals assumed to be constant. Then the distribution of X and Y between 1 and 2 must be such that both persons lie on the "contract curve",[4] CC′, if welfare is to be a maximum. For let us take any point, Q not on CC′, where 1 has OR of Y and OS of X and 2 has RB of Y and SA of X. Q lies below indifference curve IV′ of 2 (the indifference curves with primes belong to 2 and those without to 1) and below III of 1. But if 1 gives RR′ of Y to 2 and 2 gives SS′ of X to 1, they can reach Q′ on CC′ where 1 is on III and 2 is on IV′ and hence such an exchange would benefit both persons, thereby increasing welfare. It is obvious that this argument is independent of the locus of Q—so long as Q is not on CC′. It would be possible by moving along CC′ to benefit either 1 or 2 (but only at the expense of the other), depending on the direction of movement. Hence such a movement cannot be appraised on the basis of our welfare criterion.

CC′ is a locus of points which are incomparable from the welfare point of view because if we move along CC′ in either direction from any given point (Q′) we make one individual more satisfied, but make the other less satisfied. But for any given point off of CC′ there can be found some point on CC′ which is superior to it in the welfare sense.[5] And any point on CC′ will be one which is compatible with maximum welfare.

4 The "contract curve" was first used by Edgeworth. See F. Y. Edgeworth, *Mathematical Psychics*, London, 1881, pp. 25 *et seq.* It is defined as the locus of all points of tangency between the indifference curves belonging to the map of individual 1 and those belonging to the map of individual 2.

5 The exact point on CC′ that will be reached (assuming that some one point on this curve will be attained) depends upon the distribution (between individuals 1 and 2) of command over X and Y.

We may express this marginal condition of maximum welfare in the following way: *the marginal rate of substitution between any two products must be the same for every individual who consumes both.*

The second marginal condition of maximum welfare refers to

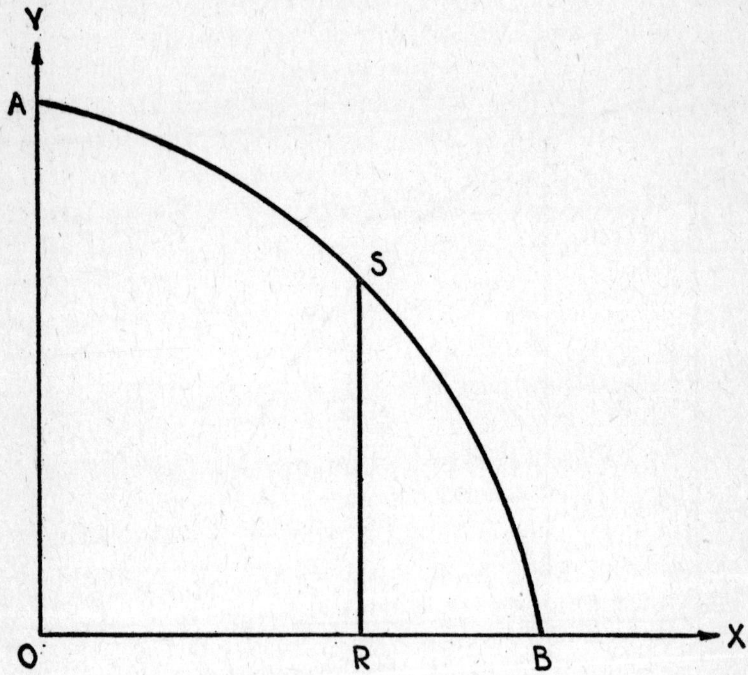

FIGURE 2

2. The Optimum Degree of Specialization

This condition of maximum welfare specifies a necessary (though not a sufficient) condition for determining the optimum output of each product by each firm. In order to determine this optimum apportionment, we have constructed figures 2 and 2a. Let AB in figure 2 represent the transformation curve between X and Y for firm 1, given the quantities of the factors it uses and of the other products it produces, and let CD in figure 2a represent the analogous curve for firm 2. Let firm 1 produce RS of Y and OR of X and let firm 2 produce OT of X and TU of Y; R, S, T and U may be any points whatever. Superimpose figure 2a on figure 2, rotating

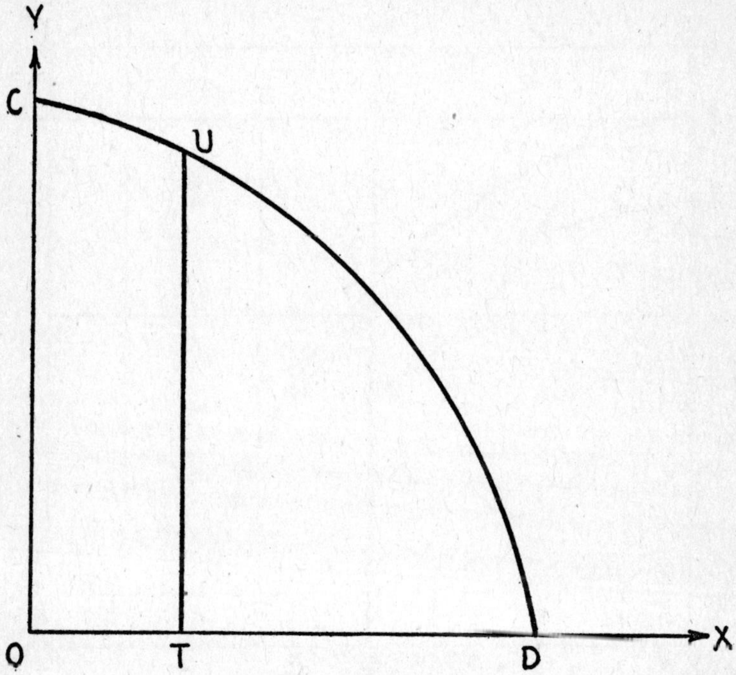

FIGURE 2a

the axes of figure 2a through a 180 degree angle and shifting the origin so that S and U coincide. The result is shown in figure 3, where summing the Y output of firm 1, RS (S indentical with U), and the Y output of firm 2, ST, we get the combined Y output of the two firms, RT; similarly, the combined X output of both firms is LF. Now let us shift the axes of firm 2 (but without rotating them) until CD becomes tangent to AB: the new position of the axes, in figure 3, is indicated by the dotted lines and the position of CD with respect to these new axes is indicated by the dotted curve C′D′, tangent to AB at P. The combined X output at P is MN>LF and the combined output of Y at P is VW>RT.

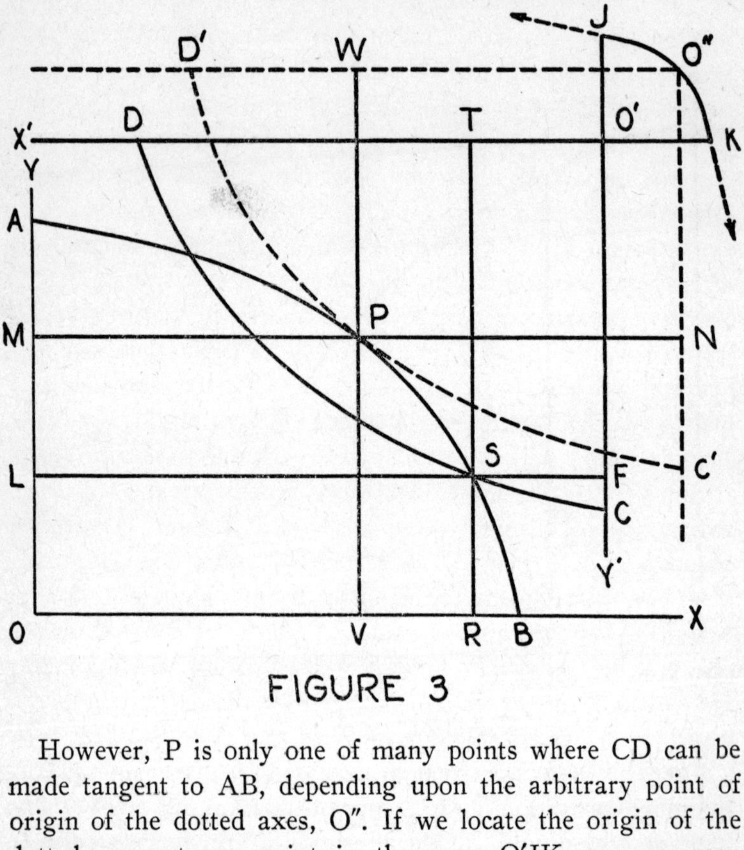

FIGURE 3

However, P is only one of many points where CD can be made tangent to AB, depending upon the arbitrary point of origin of the dotted axes, O″. If we locate the origin of the dotted axes at any point in the area, O′JK, any common point of CD and AB will, of necessity, involve a greater total output (by both firms combined) of both X and Y than if the origin were at O′. A "maximum locus", JK, may be defined by the condition that each point on JK has the property that if the origin of the dotted axes were placed there, C′D′

would be tangent to AB at one point (and have no other points in common with it.) So far as this diagram can tell us, any combination of outputs of X and Y, determined by the tangency of C′D′ and AB, may be optimal provided that O″ lies on JK. In fact the optimum position might require that O″ lie on one of the dotted extensions of JK (defined in the same way as JK); this would mean that the total output (of both firms combined) of either X or Y (as the case may be) would be less than that indicated at S and the output of the other product correspondingly larger. The optimum combination of outputs cannot be uniquely determined from this diagram alone; the diagram merely indicates a necessary condition for the optimum. This condition is that outputs must be produced in such combinations that the slopes of the transformation curves of the two firms are equal; i.e. unless the marginal rate of transformation between the two products is the same for both firms, it will always be possible to increase the combined output (by both firms taken together) of both products without changing the inputs of factors or the outputs of other products.

Since the reallocation of production between the two firms will increase the output of both X and Y without varying the output (input) of any product (factor), it will increase welfare. For the recipient (recipients) of the additional output of X and Y (or the value thereof) will be better off and no one else will be worse off. Thus if welfare is to be a maximum *the marginal rate of transformation between any two products must be the same for any two firms that produce them both.*

This particular condition of maximum welfare has had considerable application in the theory of international trade where, instead of dealing with the allocation of production between firms, the allocation of production between regions and/or countries is discussed.[6] However, this condition has a quite

6 Professor Viner has questioned the propriety of treating countries as though they were single firms. *Cf.* J. Viner, *Studies in Theory of Inter-*

general applicability in determining the optimum degree of specialization between firms or individuals. It is this condition which makes it possible, e.g. to declare that it is " inefficient " for a doctor to make his own shoes.

3. The Optimum Factor—Product Relationship

In order to maximize welfare it is necessary that the various firms mutually adapt the factors they use and the products they produce. That is, they must select their instruments of production and their intended output so that the former are technically capable of producing the latter. This may, of course, be accomplished with varying degrees of success. The optimum result will be achieved when the marginal rate of transformation of factor X into product Y (the marginal productivity of X in terms of Y) is the same for any pair of firms using X and producing Y (holding constant the quantities of all other products produced and factors used). This maximum welfare condition, and the next, together determine the most efficient method of production.

A proof of this proposition may be obtained very easily with the aid of a slight re-interpretation of figures 2, 2a and 3. The re-interpretation is that we must measure the factor units from right to left, measuring the product units in the usual way. The reason for this is that product must increase as the factor input increases and not vice-versa. However, this creates no great problem; we may take B and D as the zero points of the factor for firms 1 and 2, respectively, and proceed with the analysis as before, measuring factor input on the X axes and product output on the Y axes, and remembering to read the X axes from right to left. Then it follows that if welfare is to be a maximum the marginal rate of transformation of the

national Trade, pp. 520-26. However, T. de Scitovzsky's paper "A Reconsideration of the Theory of Tariffs," *Review of Economic Studies*, 1942, pp. 89-110, does much to surmount the difficulties involved.

factor into the product (the marginal productivity of that factor in terms of that product) must be the same for any pair of firms using the factor X and producing the product Y (holding constant the quantities of all other products produced and factors used). If the marginal rates of transformation are not the same for both firms it will be possible by transferring factor units from one firm to the other to get more product with a smaller number of factor units; a situation obviously incompatible with maximum welfare. Therefore, in order to maximize welfare, *the marginal rate of transformation between any factor and any product must be the same for any pair of firms using the factor and producing the product.*

4. The Optimum Allocation of Factors

A further re-interpretation of figures 2, 2a and 3 will enable us to develop by an analogous argument another condition of maximum welfare; this refers to the optimum utilization of factors. In order to do this we need merely measure factor quantities on both axes of figures 2 and 2a with the zero points at the intercepts of the curves and measuring from right to left and from top to bottom. This will make the curves convex to the origin (like indifference curves) when the variables are measured in the usual way. The curves will then be iso-product curves corresponding to the various combinations of factor inputs (holding quantities of all other factors and products constant).

Constructing figure 3, by manipulating the curves as before we get the following marginal condition of maximum welfare: *the marginal technical rate of substitution between any pair of factors must be the same for any two firms using both to produce the same product.*

Another condition that must be met if welfare is to be a maximum is that production must be properly directed; this is discussed in the following section.

5. The Optimum Direction of Production

The first of our marginal conditions of maximum welfare serves to determine that whatever is produced is distributed among the various consumers in a manner compatible with maximum welfare. The second, third and fourth conditions specify that whatever is produced, must be produced in the most efficient way possible. This fifth condition specifies a relationship between the technical conditions of production and the state of consumer preferences, which must be satisfied in order that welfare be maximized.

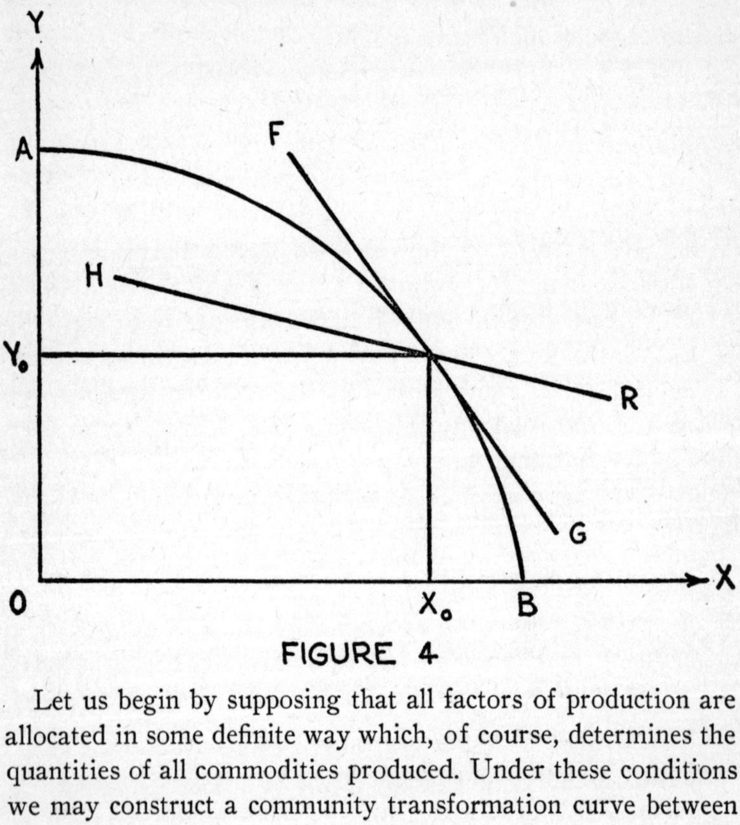

FIGURE 4

Let us begin by supposing that all factors of production are allocated in some definite way which, of course, determines the quantities of all commodities produced. Under these conditions we may construct a community transformation curve between any pair of products, X and Y; this curve gives for any quantity of Y, the maximum amount of X that can be produced, given the amounts of the other products that are produced and the supplies of the factors available. This curve is represented by AB in figure 4; its slope at any point gives the maximum additional X that can be obtained by the community if it diminishes its production of Y (and vice-versa) by a small amount, keeping its production of all other commodities constant.

Suppose that the community is producing OY_0 of Y and OX_0 of X; then the marginal rate of transformation of X into Y (and vice-versa) will be given by the slope of FG. Let us also suppose that any given individual allocates his resources between X and Y (for whatever reason) in such a way that his marginal rate of substitution, between X and Y is not given by FG, but by HR. Then, as it is technically possible for this person to substitute X for Y (at a rate given by the slope of FG) without changing the amount of any commodity consumed by any other person, (assuming that this person's indifference map is convex to the origin) such substitution will clearly make him better off (place him on a higher indifference curve) without damaging anyone else. In other words, so long as the marginal rate of substitution between any pair of products for any person is not the same as the marginal rate of transformation between the two it is technically possible to make him better off without making anyone else worse off, i.e. increase welfare. Therefore, the existence of maximum welfare implies that *the marginal rate of substitution between any pair of products for any person consuming both must be the same as the marginal rate of transformation for the community between them.*

The sixth marginal condition of maximum welfare concerns

6. The Optimum Allocation of a Factor-Unit's Time

The owner of any unit of any factor of production is always in a position to choose between using the factor to render him some kind of service directly (the kind of service depending upon the factor) and renting it out to a firm for a pecuniary reward. In any given time period, the individual has (theoretically[7]) the problem of allocating the time of the factor unit between rendering direct services and working for a money reward. (This problem occurs chiefly in connection with decisions as to the amount of time to work and the amount to spend at leisure.)

To determine the optimum allocation of a factor-unit's time, consider the following: if a moment of a factor unit's time is transferred from the rendering of direct services to its owner to aiding the production of some commodity for some firm, there will be some reward (which may vary with the commodity produced and the firm producing it) that will just compensate the factor unit's owner (leave him on the same indifference surface) for making the transfer.

This may be easily represented by an indifference map, each curve expressing the combinations of amounts of money and numbers of hours (per week) that the factor unit is used to aid in the production of a given commodity (by a given firm) among which the factor unit's owner is indifferent. And we may also construct a transformation curve between the factor unit's time spent in production and the amount of a given product produced by a given firm (given, of course, the quantities of the other factors used and products produced by the firm).

In order for welfare to be a maximum, *the marginal rate of substitution between the amount*[8] *of (product) X received for*

7 In practice, the amount of time a factor unit must work (per week) is not a matter of free choice; e. g. the work week of a laborer is set independently of his wishes and he either accepts it or does not work at all. This is one obstacle in the path of maximum welfare.

8 In order to define this condition it is convenient to assume that the factor unit's owner is rewarded in terms of the product that it aids in producing; i. e. to make this product numeraire. But this is of no significance, for we

aiding in its production (by a given firm) and the time spent in rendering this aid must be the same (for each factor unit owner) as the marginal rate of transformation between the time of his factor unit spent in aiding production (in this way) and the (product) X. To put this in somewhat simpler terms, the reward (in terms of a numeraire) that is paid the owner of a factor unit must be equal to the value (in terms of a numeraire) of the marginal physical product of the factor unit.

Non-satisfaction of this condition will make it possible to get more X by transferring a moment of a factor unit's time from the production of direct services to the production of X (or vice-versa) than would be necessary to compensate its owner (leave him on the same indifference curve) or conversely. And the extra X could be given away, thus increasing welfare. A concrete example may aid the reader in grasping the meaning of this condition. Suppose an individual is willing to perform an extra hour per day of a certain kind of work (say) housework, for a given pecuniary reward, $X. If some other individual is willing to pay a larger reward than $X, for an hour (per day) of housework, welfare will be increased if the first person performs an hour's housework (per day) for the second person. Maximum welfare requires that all such opportunities be fully exploited—which is the meaning of this sixth marginal condition of maximum welfare.

This condition must obtain between every factor unit owner and every firm (individual) to which any of its time is hired. Of course, in practice, a factor unit's time will usually be rented to only one firm.

7. Inter-temporal Conditions of Maximum Welfare

The six maximum welfare conditions set out in the pre-

are assuming implicitly (as is customary in discussion of welfare problems on this level) that all price ratios are known with certainty and exchange can be made at infinite speed and without subjective cost and hence individuals are indifferent as to the form in which they receive their rewards.

ceding sections refer to the allocation of factor services and products among individuals and firms at a given moment (or within a given period) of time. However, every firm (and individual) is confronted with another type of problem; namely the allocation of factor input and product output (of expenditure) over time. A firm may produce a given output stream with various time patterns of factor inputs and, conversely, it may have various time patterns of outputs with a given input stream of factor services.

Following Hicks,[9] we may treat the inputs or outputs of a product or factor at different moments of time as the inputs (outputs) of different products or factors. Then problems of the optimum allocation of products and factors through time become simply special cases of the more general problems of optimum allocation of products and factors; i.e. special cases where some of the products or factors may refer to different moments of time. Therefore, the six maximum welfare conditions will serve to determine the inter-temporal (as well as the "contemporaneous" [10]) allocation of all factors and products.

However, there is one inter-temporal allocation problem that does not have a counter-part in a purely contemporaneous system. That is, we must determine the proper allocation, through time, of "resource control".[11] In a contemporaneous system, resource control is simply a datum, but in an inter-temporal situation we must take into account the possibility of lending and borrowing and determine the optimum amount for each individual and firm to undertake at each moment.

9 J. R. Hicks, *Value and Capital*, Oxford University Press, 1939, pp. 193-4.

10 We refer to an economic system where all variables in the plans of individuals and firms refer to the same date, as a "contemporaneous" system —and one where the variables in the plans may have different dates as an inter-temporal one. Hicks, *op. cit.*, refers to an inter-temporal system as a dynamic one, but we prefer to save the term "dynamic" for another use.

11 By "resource control" we mean a fund of numeraire which can be used to purchase goods and services.

The determination of the optimum amount of lending or borrowing for a given firm or individual to undertake, in a given period of time, is analogous to the determination of any other optimum. It will be reached when *the marginal rate of substitution between resource control at any pair of moments* (*t_i and t_j*) *is the same for every pair of individuals or firms* (*including pairs, one member of which is a firm and the other an individual*). In other words, if individual 1 (or firm 1), at moment t_0, would give $1 for $1.03 at moment t_1 while individual 2 (or firm 2) would give more than $1.03 at t_1 for $1 at t_0, then maximum welfare requires that individual or firm 1 lend a dollar to individual or firm 2 from t_0 to t_1. We are assuming, of course, that there is no risk or uncertainty concerning the solvency of borrowers.

8. Summary of Marginal Conditions

The seven marginal conditions of maximum welfare are:

1. The marginal rate of substitution between any two products must be the same for every individual who consumes both.
2. The marginal rate of transformation between any two products must be the same for any two firms that produce both.
3. The marginal rate of transformation between any factor and any product must be the same for any pair of firms using the factor and producing the product.
4. The marginal technical rate of substitution between any pair of factors must be the same for any two firms using both to produce the same product.
5. The marginal rate of substitution between any pair of products for any person consuming both must be the same as the marginal rate of transformation (for the community) between them.

6. The marginal rate of substitution between the amount of (product) X received for aiding in its production (by a given firm) and the time spent in rendering this aid must be the same for each factor unit owner as the marginal rate of transformation between the time of his factor unit spent in aiding production (in this way) and (the product) X.
7. The marginal rate of substitution between resource control at any pair of moments (t_i and t_j) must be the same for every pair of individuals or firms (including pairs, one member of which is a firm and the other an individual).

These seven conditions may be reduced to five, if we adopt Hicks' convention of treating factors as negative products. For then, conditions 2, 3 and 4 reduce to one single condition.

It cannot be emphasized too strongly that the attainment of maximum welfare is contingent upon the simultaneous satisfaction of *all seven* of these conditions. Together they constitute a set of *necessary* conditions for the attainment of maximum welfare; but they are not *sufficient* conditions. In the first place, the marginal conditions, by themselves, do not guarantee that it is *maximum* welfare that is being attained; for all the argument we have offered thus far, it might be *minimum* welfare. To distinguish between positions of maximum and those of minimum welfare, we must consider the second order conditions of maximum welfare, assuming that the marginal (or first order) conditions are satisfied.

Assuming continuity of all preference and transformation functions and (at least) of their first and second derivatives in the neighborhood of any position where marginal conditions are satisfied, there will be a position of maximum welfare in that neighborhood *if*, and only if, all indifference curves are (in this vicinity) convex to the origin and all transformation curves are concave to it.[12] Non-satisfaction of this condition by the indifference map of any individual or the transformation function of any firm will rob the neighborhood of a welfare-maximizing position. (It could be a position of minimum welfare only if all indifference curves were more concave to the orgin than the transformation curves between the same pair of products).

The convexity of the indifference curves implies nothing new to students of economics; it is merely the familiar assumption that each consumer has a diminishing marginal rate of substitution between each pair of commodities.[13] And the concavity of the transformation curves reflects merely the familiar assumption that there is a diminishing marginal rate of transformation between any product and any factor—or any pair of products—given the quantities of all other factors used and products produced by the given firm.[14]

But even if the second-order maximum conditions are also satisfied, the satisfaction of the marginal conditions is not sufficient to guarantee maximum welfare. For there is yet another set of conditions which must be satisfied in order that welfare be a maximum. Professor Hicks calls these conditions, the total conditions; they state, inter alia, that if welfare is to be a maximum, it must be impossible to increase welfare by producing a product not otherwise produced (or produced by only one firm); or by using a factor not otherwise used (or used by only one firm). Where welfare can be increased by such operations, the optimum position obviously is not determined uniquely by the marginal conditions; i.e. there is more than one

12 To be quite precise, maximum welfare requires merely that all indifference curves in the area be less concave to the origin than the transformation curves (between the same pair of products).

13 *Cf.* J. R. Hicks, *Value and Capital,* Oxford University Press, 1939, Chapter II.

14 *Cf.* J. R. Hicks, *op. cit.*, Chapter VI.

maximum position and one of the maxima lies where the output (input) of a product (factor) by a firm and/or consumption of a product by a consumer is zero.

It is possible for the marginal conditions to be satisfied without the total conditions being satisfied. For example, a product might not be produced at all whose production would increase welfare, even though all products that were produced satisfied the marginal and second-order conditions.

Strictly speaking, the whole set of maximum welfare conditions may be stated in terms of the total conditions. Such a statement would be as follows: if welfare is to be a maximum, it must be impossible to increase it by varying the output of any product by any firm (including variations from zero); by varying the amount of any product consumed by any consumer (including variations from zero); or by varying the amount of any factor unit used to yield direct service to any individual (including variations from zero). This verbose and uninformative statement contains implicitly all the marginal conditions; in fact, we have deduced, implicitly, these latter conditions from this more general one. However, the marginal conditions, although they follow from this obvious general condition, are not altogether obvious in their implications (as will be seen), and hence we have followed the usual procedure of developing them in detail.

If the marginal, second-order and total conditions are all satisfied, welfare will be a maximum. But this maximum is not unique; for it pre-supposes a given distribution of income (measured in terms of a numeraire) that is not determined by the conditions of maximum welfare. So far as these conditions are concerned, the distribution of income is arbitrary; but changes in the distribution will (except for flukes) cause variations in the welfare-maximizing outputs of the various products and allocations of the various factors.

Having set out the conditions of maximum welfare, let us now see what use can be made of them.

CHAPTER III

PERFECT COMPETITION AND THE ATTAINMENT OF MAXIMUM WELFARE

THE bouquets that economists have thrown at the institution of laissez-faire have been so profuse that it has long seemed, to many critics, as though economists (with a few honorable exceptions) constituted an idolatrous cult. But as in many another religion, the actual doctrine was more involved than its dogma indicated. The worship, if you like, of laissez-faire was never (at least among economists we like to remember) unconditional; it was always based on the (often explicit) assumption that laissez-faire would usher in, or at least be accompained by, "free competition." But, to many critics, "free" competition—or any other kind—has no particular virtues, and the economist has had—and still has—to wage a vigorous battle in its defense. However, the economist's idea of competition has undergone a considerable change: he has been forced to define competition in an increasingly rigorous manner until, in the last decade, the vague "absence of monopoly" has become the relatively precise concept of pure—or perfect—competition.[1] But all the virtues of the older and vaguer idea of competition also adhere to these newer and more precise concepts. Just as the "Classical" economists of 100 years ago agitated for the removal of barriers to "free competition" by establishing laissez-faire, so today, many economists demand positive action to attain, wherever possible, pure competition. The modern economist's [2] program of action

1 Pure and perfect competition are by no means identical concepts and will be distinguished below.

2 Of course, not all modern economists are lovers of competition; far from it. However, there is a notable, numerous and highly articulate group who are.

differs greatly from that of a "classical" economist—and he is much less optimistic, but his ideas as to the proper objectives of economic policy remain basically those of his classical predecessors. In this chapter, we shall attempt to provide an explanation, in part at least, of the continuous intellectual attraction that the idea of competition has had for the students of economics.

The peculiar property of competition that makes it seem so attractive is really (as we shall see) a property of perfect competition only. To be specific, under conditions of perfect competition, all of the marginal (and the second-order) conditions of maximum welfare will be satisfied.

1. Perfect Competition and the Marginal Conditions

The proof of this is, fortunately, quite simple. Let us take each marginal condition separately and in the order listed in section 8 of the preceding chapter.

1. Since, under conditions of perfect competition, the price of each product is independent of the quantity any one consumer buys, the consumer bent on maximizing his satisfaction,[3] will make the marginal rate of substitution between any pair of products equal to the ratio of their prices. Therefore, as the price of any product is, under perfect competition, the same to every purchaser of it, each consumer (consuming both members of any pair of products) will, in maximizing his satisfaction, make his marginal rate of substitution between the two products the

3 We assume throughout that each individual and firm behaves rationally; i.e. that every individual tries to maximize his satisfaction and every firm tries to maximize its profits. Since in this chapter we are assuming perfect knowledge (implicit in the concept of perfect competition), we also assume that there is no cost, in terms of effort, to the managers of the various firms, of maximizing money profits. In the real world such costs exist and may require a modification of this customary assumption. *Cf.* T. de Scitovzsky, "A Note on Profit Maximization and its Implications," *Review of Economic Studies*, Winter, 1943, pp. 57-60 and see Chapter VII, pp. 86-8.

same as that of every other consumer (who consumes both products). Thus, if there is perfect competition the first marginal condition will be satisfied.

2. Under conditions of perfect competition, each producer makes the marginal rate of transformation (given the quantities of all factors hired and of all other products produced) between any pair of products, X and Y, equal to the ratio of their prices. For if this equality did not hold, it would be possible to increase profits by producing one unit more of X and one unit less of Y (or vice versa). Therefore, since perfect competition implies that every firm selling a given product receives the same price for it, any firm that produces both members of a given pair of products will have the same marginal rate of transformation between them as any other. Hence the existence of perfect competition implies that the second marginal condition of maximum welfare will be satisfied.
3. Under perfect competition each firm makes the marginal rate of transformation between any factor and any product equal to the ratio of their prices. Following Hicks, we may treat a factor as a negative product, and thus make the proof of this theorem identical with that of the preceding one.
4. Given perfect competition, the individual firm, in order to maximize its profits will make the marginal (technical) rate of substitution between any pair of factors equal to the ratio of their prices.[4] Hence, because of the uniformity of factor prices to all purchasers under conditions of perfect competition, the marginal (technical) rate of substitution between any pair of factors will be the same to any firm using both.
5. As is quite well known, under conditions of perfect competition, the individual firm maximizes its profits by pro-

4 *Cf.* J. R. Hicks, *Value and Capital*, Chapter VI.

ducing at the rate that makes marginal cost equal to price. Choose commodity X as numeraire: then if the marginal cost of Y (in terms of X) is equal to the price of Y (in terms of X) and similarly for Z, U, W etc. (in terms of X) then the ratio of the marginal costs of producing any pair of products must be the same as the ratio of their prices. The marginal rate of transformation of Y into Z (Y and Z being any products) must be the same as the ratio of their marginal costs (if the system is to be in equilibrium under perfect competition); because if it were not, then entrepreneurs could, by transforming one into the other, increase their profits. Thus, under perfect competition, the marginal rate of transformation between any pair of products must be the same as the ratio of their prices.[5] But since we have already seen that, under perfect competition, each consumer (consuming both products) makes the marginal rate of substitution between

5 A critical reader might well ask if this statement would not be true, even if the marginal cost of producing each product were not equal to its price, but merely if the ratio of the price of every product to its marginal cost were the same? The answer is yes, if we include direct services of factors as products; but if the ratio of the price of every product (including direct services) to its marginal cost is the same, then the marginal cost of producing each product must be equal to its price. For the ratio of price to marginal cost of any product, X, in terms of any other product, Y, is the reciprocal of that ratio for Y in terms of X. The only value of the two ratios which makes them equal is unity; i. e. the only possible ratio of price to marginal cost which could hold for *all* products simultaneously is unity. Therefore if the ratio of price to marginal cost is the same for all products, price must equal marginal cost for each of them.

If the direct services of factors were not included as products in the above proposition, then making the ratio of price to marginal cost the same for all products would not imply the attainment of maximum welfare. For then the price of a product in terms of the time of a factor-unit would be other than the marginal cost (marginal rate of transformation) of that product in terms of that factor unit's time, which violates the sixth marginal condition of maximum welfare.

The same point is also made by A. P. Lerner, *op. cit.*, pp. 100-05.

each pair of products equal to the ratio of their prices, it follows that, under perfect competition, the marginal rate of substitution between any pair of products will be the same to every individual (consuming both) as their marginal rate of transformation. Thus perfect competition implies the satisfaction of the fifth marginal condition of maximum welfare.

6. Under perfect competition, each firm will hire any factor service, Y, in the quantity that makes the value of its marginal physical product equal to its price.[6] Similarly, in order to maximize profit, each firm will hire each factor unit a number of hours (per week) that makes the value of the marginal physical product of an hour of that factor unit's time equal to its price per hour. If we make the product in question the numeriare, the value of the marginal physical product of a factor unit's time becomes identical with the marginal rate of transformation between the factor unit's time spent in aiding production and the product in question.[7]

However, perfect competition also implies that the owner of a factor unit, in order to maximize his satisfaction, will make the marginal rate of substitution between the money (numeraire) received for letting his factor unit, Y, aid in the production of a given product, X, (by a given firm), and the time spent in rendering direct services to himself, equal to the unit's money rate of reward.[8]

6 *Cf.* Joan Robinson, *The Economics of Imperfect Competition*, Macmillan, 1934, Chapter 21.

7 Under conditions of perfect competition, a unit of any one commodity, Z, is, from the point of view of an individual, merely a given multiple of a unit of any other, X, as he may exchange one for the other at a given rate. Therefore, it is a matter of complete indifference as to which commodity we treat as numeraire.

8 This proposition may seem a bit unfamiliar, but actually it is a rather simple variant of the condition for the consumer's equilibrium. Let one axis

Thus, perfect competition makes the marginal rate of substitution to the owner of each factor unit between receipts of X (or its exchange equivalent in numeraire) and factor unit Y's time spent in rendering him direct service, equal to the marginal rate of transformation between Y's time spent in aiding production (in this way) and the amount of X produced. It therefore implies the satisfaction of the sixth marginal condition of maximum welfare.

7. Under perfect competition each firm and individual will lend or borrow funds between any two moments of time until the marginal rate of substitution between resource control (measured in terms of a numeraire) at the two moments is the same as the ratio of a dollar (or any convenient numeraire unit) at the earlier date to a dollar plus accumulated interest at the later date. Since, under perfect competition, the rate of interest (on a "riskless secur-

---

of the indifference map (say the vertical one) with which the factor owner is confronted, represent minutes per time period (e. g. per week) that the factor unit is *not* hired out; and let the other measure the money reward received for hiring out the factor unit to a given firm. Each indifference curve indicates a given level of satisfaction corresponding to various quantities of money earned by the factor unit and time spent in rendering direct service to its owner. (In the neighborhood of the equilibrium position, at least, the indifference curves must be convex to the origin.) The intercept of the analogue of the "budget line" on the vertical axis will indicate the total number of minutes in a week, and its intercept on the horizontal axis the amount of money (numeraire) the factor unit could earn if it were hired out for every minute of the week. The co-ordinates of that point on the "budget line" where it contacts the highest indifference curve will give the number of minutes (per week) that the factor unit is *not* hired out and the amount of money that it earns per week.

The slope of the "budget line" measures the reward per unit of time that the factor receives for working for a given firm. It is this rate of reward, to which the owner of the factor unit equates the marginal rate of substitution between the factor unit's money earnings and time it spends in rendering direct service to himself. (While this argument has been developed on the assumption that the factor unit can be "hired out" to only one firm in a given week, this assumption is not necessary and can be abandoned.)

ity") will be the same for all individuals and firms, perfect competition guarantees the satisfaction of the seventh marginal condition.

If the level of satisfaction attained by any of the consumers, or the profits earned by any of the firms were a minimum and not a maximum they would immediately change their behavior. Therefore the attainment of stable equilibrium under conditions of perfect competition implies the satisfaction not only of the marginal conditions of maximum welfare, but of the second order conditions as well.

The sceptical, however, may well ask if a position of maximum welfare is, in fact, possible of attainment. To answer that if there is perfect competition in all markets, the attainment of a position of stable equilibrium implies the attainment of maximum welfare transforms, but does not answer, the question. For it is very unlikely that perfect competition (or a reasonable approximation thereto) is possible of attainment in every market.[9]

2. The Possibility of Attaining Perfect Competition

In fact, as soon as it is carefully defined, it becomes apparent that perfect competition (in the strict sense of the term) is unattainable. For perfect competition requires not only 1. that any one buyer (seller) buys (sells) only an infinitesimal part of the total amount of any one commodity bought (sold) during any given period of time, but also 2. that every commodity (including factors of production) is infinitely divisible and infinitely mobile (i.e. that it can be moved and installed with infinite speed and with zero transportation and installation cost) and 3. that every consumer and entrepreneur has perfect

9 Of course, it is possible that maximum welfare might be attained by appropriate governmental intervention without perfect or even pure competition; this possibility will be discussed in the next three chapters.

knowledge.[10] Conditions 2 and 3 are obviously incapable of satisfaction.

But our argument concerning the satisfaction of the marginal conditions of maximum welfare has not involved all of the properties of perfect competition. It needs only that 1. every individual and firm buy or sell such a small part of the total amount of any commodity that the effect of purchases or sales on the price is negligible and is hence ignored and 2. that the price of any commodity is the same to all buyers and sellers. These two conditions are tantamount to what Chamberlin [11] calls "pure competition" and are obviously less difficult of satisfaction than those of perfect competition.

It might seem therefore that in order to attain maximum welfare it would be sufficient to have "pure competition" and that the more exacting requirements of "perfect competition" could be ignored. However, this is not true; the difficulty of attaining maximum welfare without "perfect knowledge" is shown in Chapter VI and throughout Book II. And last, but far from least, indivisibilities in the factors of production may be sufficient to make maximum welfare incompatible with pure competition.

Indivisibilities cause trouble in that where they exist the marginal (and second-order) conditions cease to be sufficient to define a position of maximum welfare. This will be explained in detail in the next chapter.

10 *Cf.* E. H. Chamberlin, *The Theory of Monopolistic Competition,* Harvard University Press, 3rd edition, 1938; Chapter I.

11 E. H. Chamberlin, *op. cit*

CHAPTER IV

AN OBSTACLE TO THE ATTAINMENT OF MAXIMUM WELFARE: MONOPOLY

I. MIS-ALLOCATION OF RESOURCES: THE ECONOMIST'S COMPLAINT

Monopolies and their possessors have long been regarded with suspicion and distrust. The popular feeling is that the monopolist, by reason of his special position, manages to secure an unduly large share of the national income by charging extortionate prices. More recently, there has been considerable agitation against monopolies on the ground that, by following restrictive output and price policies, they cause unemployment. There may be considerable foundation for both beliefs, and economists have argued in support of one complaint or the other, or both.

However, there is still another complaint against "Monopoly"; it causes a mis-allocation of productive resources. But this complaint is almost exclusively a complaint of the professional economist; indeed, the lay public is scarcely aware of the existence of a resource allocation problem, let alone the role of the pricing system in its solution, and the implications of "Monopoly" in connection with it. Nonetheless, it is with this aspect of "Monopoly" that we shall deal in the present chapter. First let us make clear what we mean by the term "Monopoly".

In recent years, economists have come to think of Monopoly and Competition, not as mutually exclusive categories, but rather as polar opposites. No longer is a firm thought to be either a "Monopolist" or a "Competitor," but is very likely to be considered a little of both.

A firm is at the pole of competition, if it is a pure competitor; i.e. if it sells (or buys) such a small portion of the total amount sold (bought) in any market in which it deals that it cannot affect the price of the commodity. If the firm is a pure competitor in a particular market it will, in the course of maximizing its profits, produce that output which makes the marginal cost of producing the commodity in question equal to its price. However, if in any particular market a firm finds that, by varying the amount that it sells, it can affect the market price, it will, in maximizing its profits, take this fact into account in determining its output. That is, the marginal revenue of selling output will be less than price and hence maximizing profits (marginal cost = marginal revenue) will make marginal cost less than price. Unless otherwise specified, any firm that can maximize its profits by keeping price above marginal cost will be referred to as a "Monopolist"; other firms are, of course, pure competitors.

If all firms were pure competitors the fifth marginal condition of maximum welfare would be satisfied.[1] However, the existence of Monopolistic firms causes a violation of this condition and consequently a "mis-allocation of resources." If the state is to use its power to maximize welfare, it would seem obvious, at first blush, that it should intervene and compel each firm to produce that output which makes marginal cost equal to price. But this is easier said than done.[2] For, imposing this rule upon firms that would not maximize their profits by following it, might make it impossible for them to cover their total costs and thus make subsidies ultimately necessary in order to keep them in business. In other words, if marginal cost is made equal to price, average cost may exceed price and the enterprise may not be self-supporting. This has certain implications for welfare that require examination. But before

1 See above, pp. 41-42.

2 Let us waive the objection that it would be administratively difficult because most firms have no very definite idea as to the shape of their cost function.

we begin let us make clear that the analysis of the following section is based on the assumption that apart from the firm or product under consideration, *all* conditions of maximum welfare are satisfied; i.e. the analysis is of the partial equilibrium variety. A general equilibrium analysis is offered in the third section of this chapter.

2. MAXIMUM WELFARE AND STATE INTERVENTION TO MAKE PRICE EQUAL MARGINAL COST

So long as there is some output, X_1, of a given commodity, X, such that the algebraic sum of the compensating taxes and bounties (that could be levied and collected as a result of varying the output of X from zero to X_1) is positive, maximum welfare requires that some quantity of X be produced. Unfortunately, however, this does not imply that there is a market price, yielding a revenue sufficient to cover the total cost of producing X_1. It may be that it would require a perfectly discriminating monopolist (who exacts a payment for each unit exactly equal to the amount of the numeraire that the purchaser could give up and be as well off as if he had not purchased that unit) to exact a sufficient amount of revenue to cover the total cost of production. If a perfectly discriminating monopolist could only just cover his total cost at his profit maximizing output, then it is a matter of indifference, from the welfare point of view, as to whether or not X is produced. For the purchaser of each unit of the product would be charged a price equal to the maximum amount he would be willing to pay for the unit rather than do without it. Thus no consumer would be made better (or worse) off because of the production, and since the monopolist is just covering his total cost, he is no better (or worse) off because of the production, either; welfare would therefore be unaffected by the production. But if the perfectly discriminating monopolist could more than cover his total costs at some output, then he would be made better off by producing this output, while no one else would be made worse off, and thus welfare would be increased.

Indeed the monopolist might increase welfare by pursuing a policy of perfect discrimination if he cannot (or will not) make marginal cost equal to price.[3] For if there is any consumer who would be willing to pay a price for an extra unit of a commodity in excess of its marginal cost, welfare will be increased if the unit is produced and sold to that consumer. If all possibilities of increasing welfare in this manner are exhausted, the marginal cost of producing this commodity will be equal to the amount of a compensating tax that could be levied on each consumer (who consumes any of it) if he were given an extra unit of it. If we compute both the compensating tax and the marginal cost in terms of the numeraire, it follows that exhausting all possibilities of increasing welfare in the above manner implies the satisfaction of the fifth marginal condition of maximum welfare.[4]

Making marginal cost equal to price (for all consumers) is one way of attaining the above relationship and it is this fact that gives "welfare significance" to the idea that marginal cost should be equal to price. (One advantage of making marginal cost equal price, as compared with perfect discrimination, is that the former facilitates the satisfaction of the first marginal condition as well as the fifth, while the latter does not.)

But whatever might be said for (or against) perfect dis-

3 Of course, the more successfully a monopolist discriminates, the greater will be his real income and (perhaps) the smaller, those of his customers. However, if compensating taxes and bounties are collected and paid, a price policy of perfect discrimination will increase welfare over one of simple (undiscriminating) monopoly.

4 Price discrimination may, of course, involve the violation of the first marginal condition, but it will not always do so. For example, in the case of medical services (or other services) which cannot be exchanged between persons the first marginal condition has no meaning.

crimination in theory, it is, in practice, impossible of attainment. Therefore, if total costs cannot be covered by making marginal cost equal to price, without price discrimination, the price will be kept sufficiently far above marginal cost to make it profitable to produce the commodity. In such cases, welfare economists [5] have recommended either, that the government purchase the firm producing this commodity and run it on a welfare maximizing basis, or that it regulate the firm so that it produces an output such as to make marginal cost equal to price, paying the firm a subsidy sufficient to cover its overhead cost. In either case (analytically they are the same), the government's action is justified on welfare grounds, as can be seen from the following: assume that the government charges a price equal to the marginal cost of the equilibrium output, but restricts actual output to that which would have been produced by the monopolist and supplies each customer only the amount that he previously purchased. The government can then pay the monopolist the same total revenue he would have received from the unhampered use of his monopoly, the revenue being derived from sales of the product plus the proceeds of a tax levied upon each of the customers equal to the difference between what he pays to the government (when price equals the marginal cost of the equilibrium output) and what he would have paid to the monopolist had the government not intervened. Thus, without harming any *other* individual (taxpayer) the government can collect, in compensating taxes, sufficient revenue to compensate the monopolist for any loss born in making price equal to marginal cost of the equilibrium output—*providing output is restricted to the level that would have maximized the monopolist's profit.* But allowing output to expand freely to the equilibrium level where (marginal cost = price) cannot re-

5 *Cf.* Harold Hotelling, "The General Welfare in Relation to Problems of Taxation and of Railway and Utility Rates," *Econometrica,* July, 1938, pp. 242-69. This is the classic treatment of this subject; but see also A. P. Lerner, "Statistics and Dynamics in a Socialist State," *Economic Journal,* June, 1937, and "The Economics of Control," Chapter 16.

duce either welfare or profits and will almost certainly increase both. For if the demand curve is continuous and has a finite elasticity, then the purchasers of the units in excess of the amount that the monopolist would produce can pay a positive compensating tax. And so long as the demand curve does not lie below the average prime cost curve at any output over the relevant range (which will be the case in any stable situation) the extra revenue received for the extra output will at least equal the extra cost of producing it; and if the average prime cost curve has a positive slope, (which it will if we rule out neutral equilibrium) the extra revenue will exceed the extra cost thus adding to profits. Thus the government can increase welfare, by renting a monopoly from its owner and operating it so as to make marginal cost equal price. That this is a welfare-maximizing policy (i.e. making price equal to marginal cost) follows directly from the previous argument.[6]

When economists urge, on the basis of the above argument, that the state "take over" private monopolies and run them so as to make marginal cost equal to price they have the so-called "natural monoplies" in mind. That is, their policy recommendations are usually intended to apply to public utilities, railroads, bridges, perhaps certain types of heavy manufacturing, etc. The characteristic feature of these so-called natural monopolies is that they could produce a larger output at a lower average cost than that at which they can produce their profit maximizing output. This is because their maximum technical efficiency is reached at an output larger than that which is most

6 It might happen that there would be no single price at which total costs could be covered and the commodity could be produced at a profit only if there was a certain amount of discrimination, which might be impossible of attainment in practice. Under these conditions the commodity will not be produced unless the state intervenes, and either engages in production on its own account or subsidizes a private firm to do so. The ideal output will, of course, be that which makes marginal cost equal to price. This case is, in principle, identical with that discussed in the text (where the firm could cover its total costs); the inability of the firm to cover its total costs is irrelevant to this problem.

profitable to them. When this situation exists there is said to be "excess capacity."

However, this situation exists all over the economy. The much criticized inefficiency of the distributive system, "too many stores"; "too many brands"; etc. is merely the result of the fact that most retail distributing agencies (grocery stores, gasoline stations, etc.) could "produce" (distribute) more of any given product, in any given period of time, at a lower average cost than that which they incur in distributing the most profitable amount. This is because distributive firms are technically most efficient at greater "outputs" than those most profitable to them.

As Triffin[7] has shown, a completely general equilibrium theory requires that we begin by assuming that each firm produces one or more products, over each of which it has a complete monopoly. The products produced by the various firms have relations of substitution and complementarity and thus their prices and outputs are inter-related. When the elasticity of substitution between two products of the same or different firms becomes infinite, the two products become one, i. e. they are the same product; if a sufficiently large number of firms produce the same product, so that 1. the cross elasticity of demand for the product of one of the competing firms with respect to the price charged by any one of the others is infinite, and 2. the cross elasticity of the price charged by any one firm with respect to the output of any one of the others is zero, there is said to be pure competition.

WELFARE AND THE PROBLEMS OF MONOPOLISTIC COMPETITION, OLIGOPOLY, ETC.

Viewed in this light, most firms are monopolists of most of the products they produce; slight variations in location, quality,

7 Robert Triffin, "Monopolistic Competition and General Equilibrium Theory," Harvard University Press, 1940, pp. 97 *et seq.* Also M. W. Reder, "Monopolistic Competition and the Stability Conditions," *Review of Economic Studies*, Feb., 1941, pp. 122-5.

design, branding or packaging of the product may and do cause the elasticities of substitution between the outputs of closely competitive firms to be less than infinite.[8] Therefore there is no " essential " difference between the " natural " monopolies and the ordinary " competitive " advantages of superior location, packaging, etc. The difference lies merely in the size of the elasticity of substitution between the output of the firm in question and that of its competitors; the " natural " monopoly, e. g. a Gas and Electric Company, usually has a rather low elasticity of substitution between its products and those of its nearest competitors, while the " corner " grocery store, for example, has a very high elasticity of substitution between its products and those of the grocery store " down the street " (which are identical save for location).

The practical implications of this are rather serious. It means that if the state is to pursue a policy of maximizing welfare, it will be compelled to intervene with many, perhaps most, firms: e.g. it will be required to subsidize them in order that they be able to cover their total costs while making marginal cost equal to price. The reader might well ask if the pursuit of maximum welfare is, in such cases, really worth the trouble. Formally the answer is quite simple; if the tax cost of administering such a regulation is less than the algebraic sum of the compensating taxes that could be collected on account of the increase in welfare resulting from its enforcement, then maximum welfare is " worth " the pursuing. If the tax cost exceeds this amount, then the reverse is true. The practical implications of these statements are worthy of detailed consideration, but we cannot enter into them here.

Now let us consider the welfare implications of those cases where there is competition beween firms producing an identical product, but where there is not a sufficient number of firms to establish pure competition. These are the cases of duopoly,

8 This is an old story to those familiar with the literature of Monopolistic Competition; *cf.* particularly E. H. Chamberlin, *op. cit.*

triopoly, oligopoly, etc. As is well known, the equilibrium outputs and prices of the various firms, under these conditions, are formally indeterminate unless further specification is made concerning the shapes of the "reaction curves." But the equilibrium position may very well be such that it will be possible for the state to increase welfare by allocating the equilibrium output among the various firms in such a way as to reduce the total cost of producing it. The state will be able to increase welfare further if it can set a price such that the market is just cleared when each firm produces an output which makes its marginal cost of production equal to that price.

These welfare-increasing operations of the state may or may not involve a decrease in the number of firms. It may be that maximum welfare requires that the output of some firms be increased while that of others be contracted to the point where their total cost is less than the total revenue they could derive from perfect discrimination, in which case they should, from the welfare point of view, be eliminated. For example, if firm A has an average cost curve which lies above that of firm B at every output, and if firm A can produce the entire welfare maximizing output while operating on the falling branch of its average cost curve, welfare would be increased by eliminating firm B.

In order to decide whether any firm of any kind ought to be created (or not destroyed in the long run) on welfare grounds we need merely determine whether there is some output of the firm at which it could cover its total cost (by perfect discrimination, if necessary) and leave a profit; if there is, then welfare considerations demand that the firm exist, if not, then they imply either (1) that it ought not to exist, if at all outputs, it would take a loss (even with perfect discrimination) or (2) that its existence is a matter of indifference if, at some output it would (with perfect discrimination) just cover total costs. The same criterion can be applied to the determination of whether a firm should produce a given product (including, of course, new varieties of the "same" product), add a new plant, etc.[9] It should be noted that questions as to whether welfare

9 Usually in discussions of this kind a diagram similar to figure A is used to determine the optimum size of the plant for the firm to adopt. The optimum size of plant is, given the optimum output to be OA, that defined by the curve SAC_1, as the output OA can be produced at a smaller total cost with this size plant than with any other. This can be seen from the tangency of the SAC_1 curve (the average cost curve for the firm with that size plant) to the LAC curve the ordinates of which give the minimum

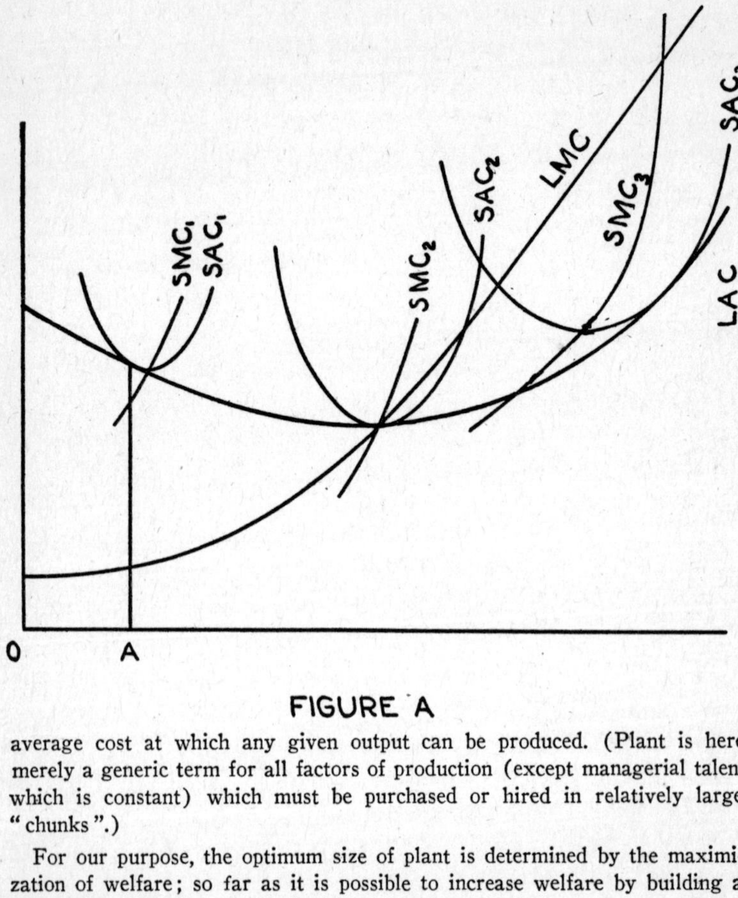

FIGURE A

average cost at which any given output can be produced. (Plant is here merely a generic term for all factors of production (except managerial talent which is constant) which must be purchased or hired in relatively large "chunks".)

For our purpose, the optimum size of plant is determined by the maximization of welfare; so far as it is possible to increase welfare by building a larger plant, the size of the plant should be increased, but no further. (Thus the optimum size plant need not be that whose short-run average cost curve is SAC_2.) We are assuming that there is a choice of building one size plant

would be increased by increasing (decreasing) the size of a firm, varying the quality of a product etc. are, from the analytical point of view, simply questions as to whether welfare can be increased by scrapping one plant and constructing another of a different size; by ceasing the production of one product and commencing that of another, etc.

PARTIAL VS. GENERAL WELFARE ECONOMICS

The welfare arguments that we have developed in the preceding two sections of this chapter are partial equilibrium arguments. They refer to the optimum output of one particular product; the optimum number of firms in a particular industry etc. But, in order to determine (say) the optimum output of a particular product, we must know (inter alia) the actual outputs of other products, the quantities of the factors used in producing them, etc. If all of these are the welfare maximizing quantities, then the welfare maximizing output of the particular product will be that which makes the marginal cost of producing it equal to its price.

However, this will not be true, if (as is in fact the case) there are fairly wide-spread and extensive divergences of actual from optimum product outputs and factor inputs due to monoply and/or monopsony. For when such divergences exist, firms will, in restricting output to the point where marginal cost equals marginal revenue (where marginal revenue is less than price), reduce the aggregate demand for each of the various factors at given prices and thus reduce their equilibrium prices. Thus each firm will find the ordinates of its marginal cost curve lying below the levels they would have, if every other firm were producing its welfare maximizing output. [If an appreciable number of firms have monopsony power over one (or more) factors, this effect will be intensified.]

If a particular firm should happen to be a pure competitor,

---

or another, and that no plant has yet been constructed. Throughout this chapter we assume, except when otherwise stated, that there are no fixed commitments, i. e. we are dealing with long run adjustments.

it would, under these circumstances, produce an output in excess of that which it would produce if welfare were a maximum. A monopolistic firm will produce more or less than the welfare maximizing output depending upon the elasticity of its demand curve; it might even, if by accident its demand curve should have the appropriate shape, produce exactly the welfare maximizing quantity.

If it is known that the output of every product other than X is at its optimum value, then it is possible to say that if the output of X is such that the price of X exceeds its marginal cost to some firms, then those firms should increase their output of X. But if monopoly and/or monopsony is widespread, there is no easily applied rule that enables us to determine whether or not the output of a particular commodity is too large or too small. The general rule for determining whether the output of X is too large (small) is: if the algebraic sum of the compensating taxes and bounties that could be collected on account of a unit decrease (increase) in the output of X and the corresponding increase (decrease) in the output of some other commodity, Y, is positive, then the output of X is too large (small). If the sum is negative then the output of X is too small (large). However, this rule is not easily applied. It must be realized that to say the output of commodity X is too small (from the welfare point of view) implies that the output of some other commodity, Y, (or the "leisure" of some factor-unit) is too large.[10] It would seem from the viewpoint of partial equilibrium theory, that if the price of X exceeds its marginal cost, the output of X should be expanded. But in order to increase the output of X, it is nec-

10 This may appear strange to economists accustomed to hear of "monopolistic restriction," but not of the correlative over-expansion of other industries. However, talk of "monopolistic restriction" usually assumes a background of general unemployment, while welfare economics customarily assumes (implicitly, to be sure) full employment. In Part III there is a discussion of welfare economics on the assumption of unemployed resources.

essary to decrease that of Y (or Z or W etc.) and the price of each of these might also exceed its marginal cost. Since the fifth condition of maximum welfare implies that the ratio of the prices of any pair of products to their marginal costs must be the same (assuming the absence of any consumer monopsony),[11] it might appear that X should be transformed into Y whenever the ratio of price to marginal cost is greater in the case of X than of Y (or vice-versa, if the reverse is the case). But this is not correct either, for we must consider not only X and Y, but also Z, W etc. Perhaps the output of both X and Y should be curtailed in favor of (say) W.

The optimum output of products must satisfy the fifth marginal condition for *every* pair of products and not merely for any particular pair taken in isolation. It is convenient to deal with single products in terms of the rule that marginal cost must equal price, but this rule is merely a first approximation whose validity depends upon the assumption that the entire economy adjusts itself to each output of the given commodity in such a way as to maximize welfare. If this assumption is not satisfied (and if monopoly is widespread it will not be) it is impossible to infer that a commodity is produced in less than the welfare maximizing amount merely because its price exceeds the marginal cost to any firm producing it.[12]

11 It should be remembered that the fifth marginal condition implies that the marginal rate of transformation between any pair of products must be the same as the marginal rate of substitution between them for every consumer who consumes both. The rule that price must equal marginal cost is merely an instrument for achieving this result; but it achieves it only if the consumers are not monopsonists. If they are, maximum welfare will not be attained by this rule; however, consumer monopsony is relatively unimportant.

12 We have discussed only the question of the optimum output of various products. However, analogous problems arise in connection with the proper allocation of factors of production and the allocation of each factor unit's time between the rendering of direct services and earning money income. But these are discussed in detail elsewhere, and the reader who is interested may consult A. P. Lerner, "The Economics of Control," *op. cit.*, Chapter 9-11.

Similarly, we cannot infer that a particular firm should (on welfare grounds) exist merely because the total revenue that it earns exceeds its total cost of doing business, because if the welfare maximizing output of every other product were produced, total costs might be so much higher that the firm could not cover its total costs even if it were able to engage in perfect discrimination. A similar argument applies to the question of whether or not a particular product should be produced; a particular plant constructed; etc.

In short, the prevalence of monopoly and/or monopsony makes the pricing system an imperfect instrument for directing the flow of productive instruments, or judging the effectiveness of the allocation actually made.

A PRELIMINARY ASSESSMENT OF THE CURRENT THEORY OF WELFARE ECONOMICS

Thus far we have attempted an exposition of the theory of welfare economics—and some of its more important applications—as it stands at the present time. However, we have not indicated explicitly the extent to which we accept the theory outlined. And it is rather important that we do this, since throughout the rest of the book we are rather critical of this theory.

These criticisms are not intended, and should not be interpreted, as a derogation of the admirable pioneer work of the authors cited throughout these first four chapters. These writers have given a precise, if somewhat narrow, definition of welfare and have developed in considerable detail the economic implications of making welfare (in this sense) a maximum. These implications, as we have seen, are very definite with respect to price policy; to policies for guarding competition and, by implication, free international trade; and, although we have not discussed it here, for tax policy.

However, the policy implications of the welfare criterion are developed on the basis of rather restrictive assumptions and hence they cannot be accepted, in toto, without a rather careful assessment of the appropriateness of these assumptions. We shall spend a good part of the remainder of this book making just such an assessment. But, nonetheless, given the assumptions on which it is constructed, the theory of welfare economics as it presently stands is, (with the exception noted in Chapter VIII), in our opinion, logically valid.

Thus far, we have been following a well-beaten path of economic theory. From here on the trail is by no means so well broken and, fairly often, we shall be blazing it ourselves.

CHAPTER V

FURTHER OBSTACLES TO THE ATTAINMENT OF MAXIMUM WELFARE

1. External Repercussions of Production and Consumption

In this chapter we consider a class of problems that arises to plague any government that is bent on pursuing a policy of maximizing welfare. These problems arise from the fact that the satisfaction level of a given individual, that is usually assumed to depend only upon those commodity quantities that the individual himself consumes, may actually depend, as well, upon 1. the commodity quantities produced (or the factor quantities used) by one or more firms; or upon the commodity quantities consumed by another individual, and 2. the fact that the output of a given firm may depend not only upon the factor quantities used by itself, but also upon the factor quantities used by other firms.

I. EXTERNAL REPERCUSSIONS OF PRODUCTION

One of the first instances in which a divergence between the welfare maximizing and the private profit maximizing outputs (of a given firm) was discovered, is the case where there are external repercussions of variations in the rate of output or of factor utilization by an individual firm; i.e. repercussions on other firms or individuals. We do not refer to those repercussions that affect the profits of another firm or the income of an individual via price changes; i.e. the repercussions of the behavior of a monopolist or monopsonist. Rather, we refer to purely "technical" repercussions which take place independently of price changes. As Professor Pigou[1] has discussed cases of this kind in some detail, it will suffice, for our purposes, to give only a few examples.

1 A. C. Pigou, *op. cit.*, Chapter IX.

One such example is provided by the case where a factory produces smoke as an incidental by-product, thereby harming nearby residents; i.e. increasing their laundry bills, etc. The marginal cost of the product to the producer, under these conditions, is less than the sum of the compensating bounties that would have to be paid to individuals on account of producing another unit of the product. The marginal cost born by the producer will be merely the value of the alternative product sacrificed, but the compensating bounties would have to be sufficiently greater than this to compensate those damaged by the extra smoke.

Let us designate the sum of the compensating bounties that would have to be paid on account of the production of an extra unit of output as the marginal *social* cost of that output and call marginal cost, as it is ordinarily defined, marginal *private* cost—to distinguish it from marginal social cost. (The *total* social cost of producing a given output of X is the sum of the compensating bounties necessary as a result of producing that output instead of an output of zero.) In this terminology, the previous example is simply a case where the marginal private cost curve lies below the marginal social cost curve (over the relevant range) and thus the output that (under pure competition) maximizes profits will be greater than that which maximizes welfare.

On the other hand, there are cases in which the marginal social cost curve may lie beneath the marginal private cost curve; e.g. where there are external economies of scale. A big firm, by increasing the volume of its output, and hence of its shipments, causes an extra freight train to be run thereby reducing the marginal social cost of handling shipments of other firms in the vicinity.[2]

2 In this example of external economies of scale, as in most others, it is unrealistic to treat the marginal social cost of a particular product as a continuous function of the output of another firm. External economies are usually, as here, the result of discontinuous costs which are joint to two or more firms. However, there are some cases of external economies of scale that are not altogether of this character; e. g. a firm may, by having its own

Another example is pointed out by Sir William Beveridge.[3] Where the state has a commitment to provide facilities for the rendering of various Social Services, setting up a firm in a region into which the labor supply will have to be drawn involves a cost to the government (to provide new facilities) that would not exist if the firm were established in an area where the labor supply was ready to hand.

It might be well to note that an excess or deficiency of the welfare maximizing output as compared with the profit maximizing output, due to external repercussions, might serve to counter-balance a deficiency or excess (in the opposite direction) due to the existence of monopoly. However, there is no a priori reason for assuming that such "counter-balancing" will occur.

II. EXTERNAL REPERCUSSIONS OF CONSUMPTION

The usual examples of external repercussions occur when the production function of a firm or the utility function of an individual contains the output (or factor utilization) of some other firm as one of its variables. However, there is another type of external repercussion which is rarely, if ever, recognized in discussions of welfare economics. It occurs where the utility function of one individual contains, as variables, the quantities of goods consumed by other persons.[4]

Customarily, in economic theory, it is assumed that the level of satisfaction attained by an individual depends solely upon the goods and services that *he* consumes and not upon those consumed by anyone else. This assumption is, of course, fundamental to the theory of consumer's choice and, in that connec-

employees inoculated, reduce the incidence of disease among employees of other firms and thus reduce absenteeism (in other firms) thereby increasing their profits.

3 Sir W. H. Beveridge, *Full Employment in a Free Society*, W. W. Norton and Co., New York, 1945.

4 Since the above was written, this phenomenon has been referred to by Gerhard Tintner, "A Note on Welfare Economics," *Econometrica*, January, 1946, pp. 69-78.

tion, it is a useful one. However, it has been imported into welfare economics, closely allied to the theory of consumer's choice, both logically and historically, without careful scrutiny. And it is an assumption that is, in many instances, obviously contrary to fact.

For example, a person who greatly enjoys playing tennis will be placed on a higher indifference curve if a close friend purchases a tennis racket. Some persons dislike the idea of others being in want, and hence contribute to charities; i.e. their satisfaction is increased by an increase in the amount of (say) food consumed by others. However, cases where the utility of one person is an increasing function of the quantity of goods and/or services consumed by another (or others) are without great significance for economic policy. For, if the compensating tax that could be levied on individual A due to a unit increase in the amount of product X consumed by individual B exceeds the marginal social cost (assumed equal to price) of X, then the satisfaction of individual A, as well as welfare, will be increased by A's making B a present of the given amount of X, (or more generally, contributing an amount sufficient to induce B to make the purchase), if B would not (or could not) purchase it himself. Thus unimpeded self-seeking will tend, in such cases, to maximize welfare, and thus the dependence of one individual's satisfaction on the consumption of another will not, ipso facto, make a policy of laissez-faire incompatible with the tenets of welfare economics.

However, those cases where an increase in the consumption of product by one person *diminishes* the satisfaction of another, are quite another story. These cases exist wherever "invidious expenditure" occurs. When A tries to "out-do" B (say) in the lavishness of his home, B's expenditure on house-hold furnishings puts A on a lower indifference surface. This suggests that sumptuary legislation forbidding "invidious expenditure" (if only such expenditure could be identified) might result in an increase in welfare by freeing resources from "competitive consumption" for use where they would yield greater satisfaction (given the absence of similar expenditure by others). That is, for example, the compulsory abolition of certain kinds of expensive decorations from all houses might not make anyone worse off, even if the money otherwise spent on it were taxed away; hence the proceeds of the tax could be used to increase welfare.

Proceeding on the same lines, it might be argued that a redistribution of income between rich and poor persons in favor of the poor would increase welfare, if the amounts taken from (given to) each rich (poor) man were adjusted so that the amounts taken from (given to) his social competitors were such as to leave him on the same indifference surface as before.[5] This, of course assumes that the only reason for desiring extra income is invidious (a premise, which may be questioned, but is often asserted and widely believed) and, that rich and poor, or rich, poor and middle-class, etc. are "non-competitive groups"[6] in consumption. Following this line of reasoning still further, we find that reorganizations, which would otherwise appear to increase welfare, may actually decrease it; i. e. if the benefits are distributed among socially competitive individuals in such a way as to greatly alter their competitive standings.[7]

In one sense, speculation of this kind is idle. But it has a certain value in that it should recall vividly to the mind of the economist, the relatively narrow set of assumptions within which his notions of proper economic policy are formed, and

5 Of course, it may not always be possible to do this.

6 By "non-competitive groups" we mean groups such that an increase in the consumption of any good or service by a member of one group will not diminish the satisfaction of a member of another. (Obviously the classification scheme suggested is very crude, but it would not pay, for our purposes, to refine it.)

7 This will happen if individuals on balance would rather become absolutely poorer than remain at the same level of income, but poorer relatively to certain other individuals.

remind him that slight, and not absurd, variations in those assumptions, may completely alter the conclusions which seem to follow from his analysis.

In fine, assuming that the satisfaction of one person does not depend on the consumption of any other involves the complete obscuration of all problems of prestige, jealousy etc. from the purview of our welfare criterion. This obscuration makes possible many conclusions that could not otherwise be obtained, but these conclusions must always be questioned when any policy, which would otherwise increase welfare, seems likely to disturb the relative social status of the various members of a community. A theory of welfare economics which does not take account of the importance of "keeping up with the Joneses" has a serious deficiency.

But once we start considering factors of this type, economic theory becomes so inter-twined with sociological considerations that it becomes impossible to conduct it on the usual basis of autonomy. While it is not our purpose here to discuss the propriety of conducting Economic Analysis on the assumption that Economics is an autonomous discipline, it is well to note that this book assumes, implicitly, that Economic Theory can be fruitfully discussed apart from political and sociological considerations. On the basis of this assumption, we shall assume, throughout its remainder, that the satisfaction of one individual does not depend on the consumption of another. We do not believe that, for most purposes, this assumption greatly restricts the validity of our analysis. But, nonetheless, we should keep it clearly in mind.

CHAPTER VI

ANOTHER OBSTACLE: IGNORANCE

WHEN we say that ignorance is an obstacle to the attainment of maximum welfare, we mean that even if every firm were a pure competitor and capable of covering its total costs and if there were no external repercussions of either production or consumption, the lack of perfect knowledge would still prevent the attainment of maximum welfare. To examine all of the consequences for welfare economics of abandoning the implicit assumption of perfect knowledge [1] would be an endless task. (In a sense, the whole of Part II is an elaborate discussion of the consequences of the inability of economic entities to make perfect forecasts.) In this chapter, we shall consider but one of the more important of these consequences: the existence of advertising.

I

ADVERTISING

In this section, we shall try to answer, or at least throw light on, the question of whether advertising increases welfare or the reverse. Since advertising presumably changes the demand functions of the individual consumers, it changes either their tastes or it changes the degree to which they succeed in maximizing their satisfaction. We shall consider here only the latter class of cases; i.e. the cases that result from "ignorance"; i.e. lack of perfect knowledge. (Where advertising changes tastes we cannot apply the welfare criterion we have adopted.) Assume that the individual possesses at any moment of time, a whole family of indifference maps, one for each set of his

1 It is not always appreciated how great is the reliance of welfare economics upon the assumption of perfect knowledge; in fact it is not always realized that the ordinary conclusions of welfare economics even involve this assumption. The arguments of this chapter and those of Part II will illustrate the importance of this assumption.

beliefs, prejudices, information, etc. as to the efficacy of various methods of attaining satisfaction. These maps all refer to *one* set of tastes—tastes are assumed to be constant; only the knowledge requisite to the satisfaction of the tastes varies.

The dotted indifference curve, I′, in figure 5 belongs to one of the maps corresponding to a state of knowledge which is less than perfect. The indifference curves I and II belong to the indifference map corresponding to perfect knowledge. Each point in the (X, money) plane lies on some curve in the indifference map corresponding to perfect knowledge, and hence every point on some map corresponding to less than perfect knowledge is represented also on the map corresponding to perfect knowledge; and conversely.

Let us suppose that a consumer's knowledge is such that he operates on the basis of the indifference map of which indifference curve I′ is a member. Consequently he chooses to consume OA of product X and keep OB of Money (numeraire) for other products. Now let us suppose that, due to a given expenditure on advertising by a firm producing X, the consumer represented in figure 5 acquires perfect knowledge and consequently increases his consumption of X to OC, correspondingly diminishing the amount of money kept for expenditure on other products to OD. The compensating tax that could be levied on this individual because of the advertising would be LR, as R is on the same indifference curve (of the map corresponding to perfect knowledge) as K. This means that the individual has been able to increase his satisfaction due to his new knowledge to such an extent that he would have been willing, *given this knowledge,* to pay EH (=LR) in exchange for it.[2] (Figure

2 It is necessary to emphasize that the consumer is willing, *given the additional knowledge,* to pay LR in exchange for it; for given his old knowledge (or lack of it) he would not be willing. (Figure 5 is drawn, for the sake of simplicity, on the assumption that the price of X is unchanged as a result of the advertising. This assumption, however, is not necessary for the argument.)

5 is drawn, for the sake of simplicity, on the assumption that the price of X is unchanged as a result of the advertising. This assumption, however, is not necessary for the argument.)

A given amount and kind of advertising will increase welfare if the sum of the compensating taxes that could be collected on account of the increased knowledge, (given the additional knowledge) including the extra profits of the advertiser, will exceed the total social cost of the factors used to " produce "

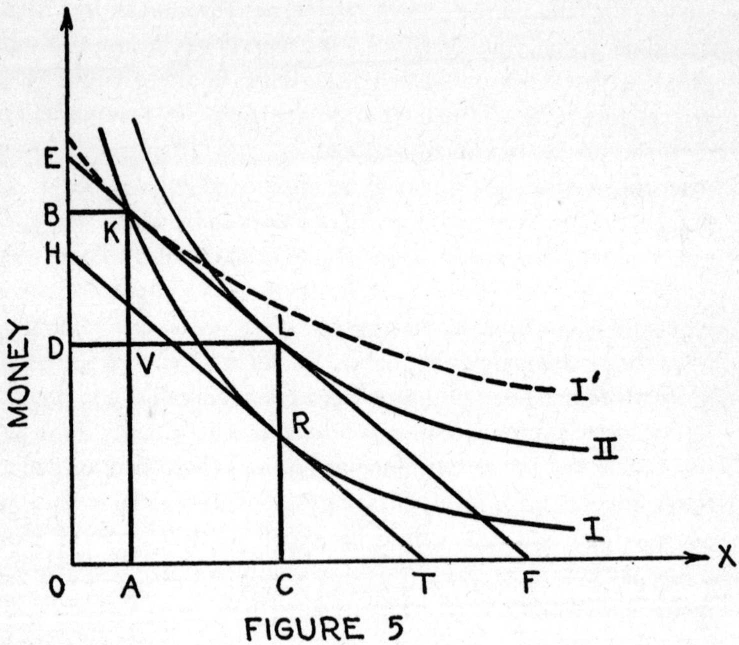

FIGURE 5

this knowledge. There is no particular reason, however, for supposing that the advertising actually undertaken will be in the welfare maximizing amounts and kinds. In fact, there is definite reason to suppose the reverse, for the marginal private and social costs of advertising certainly diverge.

Let us define the marginal social cost of advertising as the sum of the marginal social cost of the factors used and the compensating taxes (as a negative cost) and bounties that must be paid all persons in the community (except the advertiser) as a result of the advertising. Thus, if the change in knowledge increases (decreases) the welfare of the consumers then the marginal private cost curve of advertising will probably lie above (below) the marginal social cost curve over the relevent range.

The private profit maximizing amount of each "kind" of advertising that a given firm undertakes will be determined by the intersection of the marginal private cost of advertising curve [3] and the marginal advertising net revenue curve.[4] If the marginal social cost of advertising curve lies below the marginal private cost of advertising curve in the vicinity of its intersection with the marginal advertising net revenue curve, then the profit maximizing amount of advertising will be less than the welfare maximizing amount; and vice versa. If the marginal social cost of advertising curve lies above the marginal advertising net revenue curve at all points, then there should, on welfare grounds, be none of this kind of advertising.

There is, of course, no reason to expect a priori that an advertising campaign that tends to perfect knowledge will be more profitable to its initiator than one which does the reverse. It may pay some firms to increase knowledge, but it will also pay others to spread misinformation, and there is no tendency for firms in general to benefit by increasing knowledge. That is, advertising campaigns whose non-existence is required if maximum welfare is to be attained, may be privately profitable and hence undertaken; and conversely.

In determining whether or not an increase in knowledge increases or decreases welfare, it should be remembered that we must include (on the negative side) the diminution of profits of firms producing products competitive with X and (on the

3 The ordinates of this curve measure the cost of hiring the factors necessary to increase the amount of the given kind of advertising by one unit.

4 The ordinates of this curve measure the increase in the profit accruing to the firm as a result of a unit increase in its advertising—after all adjustments of output, etc. to the profit maximizing amounts have been made.

positive side) the increase in the profits of firms producing products complementary with X. It is likely, on the whole, that advertising which increases knowledge will increase welfare, but if the ratio of price minus marginal social cost to price of the products competitive with X (over the relevant range) is less than the same ratio for X (and its complements), this may not be true. For it may be that maximum welfare would be attained if less, rather than more, of X (and its complements) were consumed; but the divergence of relative marginal social costs from prices is such that, *given the existing prices,* the consumers could increase their satisfaction by consuming more X than they do in their state of less than complete knowledge.

Whether or not the advertising that is actually carried on increases welfare is, of course, a matter of guess work. Very likely some of it does and, almost certainly, some of it does not. That is, some advertising, such as that which gives accurate information regarding reputable drugs, certainly benefits consumers; probably the compensating taxes that could be levied on them, had they complete knowledge, would exceed the total social cost of the factors used in the advertising. But on the other hand, advertising that gives misleading information, particularly about drugs, damages consumers and hence will almost certainly reduce welfare. On balance, it is impossible to say, with any precision, whether the abolition of all advertising [5] would benefit or harm the community.

"Competitive advertising", i.e. advertising that is maintained simply to keep up with competitors' advertising, clearly involves a waste of resources. That is, the state, by compelling all competitors to scale down their advertising, would not diminish the knowledge of the consumers greatly, if at all, and

5 Professor J. M. Clark has called my attention to the fact that, in a world with less than perfect knowledge, the abolition of all advertising is virtually inconceivable. After all, information must be provided as to the location of places of business, the commodities offered and the prices charged. Consequently, when we speak of the abolition of "all" advertising, we refer merely to the abolition of all selling activities other than these.

would free a considerable amount of resources for use elsewhere, and would thus be very likely to increase welfare.

The growth of consumers' information services of various kinds, run on a fee basis, indicates that there is a desire for more complete knowledge which can be (and is) expressed in terms of money. It is very possible that the government, by extending and facilitating these services, could increase welfare. Advertising, insofar as it can increase welfare, is merely a substitute [6] for such services, but because of the divergence of the marginal social and private cost of advertising, it is not a particularly good substitute. Furthermore, because of the widespread scepticism of advertisers' claims, much of the genuinely beneficial advertising loses its effect, as consumers hesitate to act on the information provided; but, on the other hand, misleading advertising loses some of its ability to harm.

A well organized, independent consumers' guide, properly publicized, would be worth as much to consumers as a requirement that all advertisements be passed upon by a government board, which allowed only such advertising as would tend to the dissemination of accurate information. Besides, the quality guide would probably be much less expensive than enforcing the regulation, since the regulatory board would have to perform all the quality tests of the guide service, in addition to all its other activities. Once the guide service was well established, advertisers would either curtail their advertising to publication of the favorable rating given to their product, or would have to change the quality of their product so as to conform to the standards of the guide service.[7] Once the standards of the guide service became generally known, a producer could not get customers by making claims for his product, for the community

6 We are abstracting from any incidental benefits conferred by advertising; e. g. the benefits conferred by radio programs supported by advertising.

7 Of course, this assumes that once the consumers know the truth about various "brands" they will, given an unique price, prefer the best quality. This is not always true and when it is not, these remarks do not apply.

would not heed them unless they were backed by a high rating from the guide service; and if they were so backed, the claims would be unnecessary—the rating would be the most effective possible advertisement. This would act to restrain advertising to the welfare maximizing amount, since all advertisers would have to publicize their rating (or tacitly admit a low one) by the guide service, and hence advertising would tend to disseminate more perfect knowledge.

Another way in which the dissemination of more complete knowledge would increase welfare, is in connection with the "quality" of the various products produced. Let us assume that the "quality" of a given product may be treated as a monotonically increasing ordinal function of its total private cost of production; i.e. the "quality" of a product or brand "A" will be judged superior by all consumers (with complete knowledge) to product or brand "B" when "A" is produced in such a way that the total cost of producing "A" at all relevant outputs, is greater than that of producing "B."[8]

In figure 6 iso-revenue curves, I and II, are drawn for a firm which has the alternatives of producing any one of the products represented on the Y axis; we assume that it would be privately unprofitable to produce more than one. They indicate the various combinations of "quality" and advertising expenditure that will yield a given amount of total revenue to the firm. On the X axis is measured the amount of expenditure to be made on advertising (the expenditure to be made in the private profit maximizing way). The AB line is an iso-cost curve, representing the various combinations of expenditures on advertising and "production" that (holding the quantity produced constant) the firm has open to it, given the amount it is going to spend. Let OA (=OB) be the profit maximizing amount of expenditure; hence a point of tangency of the AB line with an iso-revenue curve determines a position of maximum private

8 Assuming of course that the output of each product or brand is produced at the lowest possible total cost for that output.

profit. Thus, the co-ordinates of the point, R, determine the

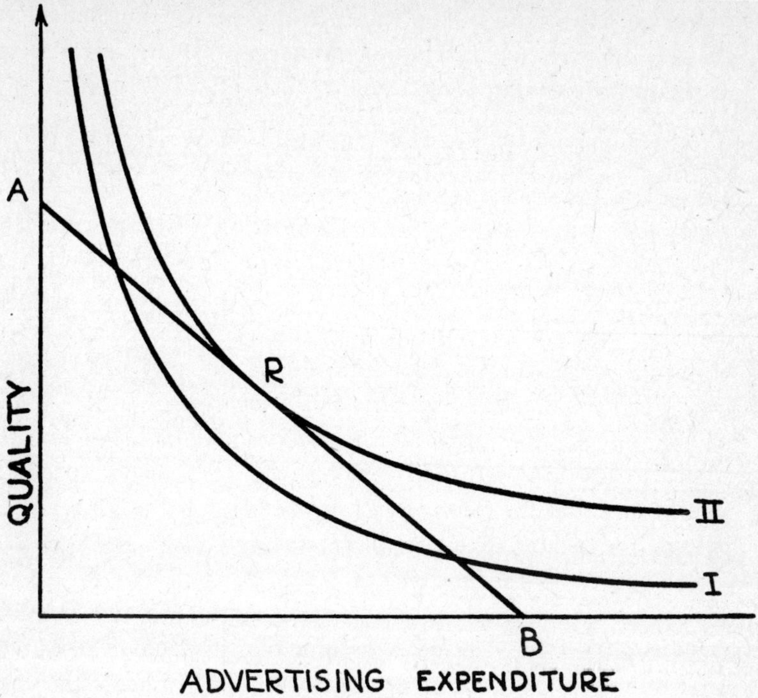

FIGURE 6

private profit maximizing expenditures on quality and advertising, respectively.

The shape of the iso-revenue curves is determined by the perfection of the knowledge of the consumers. If all consumers had perfect knowledge, the iso-revenue curves would be parallel to the X axis, indicating that the demand curve for the firm's output could not be shifted by advertising,[9] but only by improving the quality of the product. In this case, the profit maximizing expenditure on advertising would be zero. Situations of this sort are approximated when the product is of the sort

9 This would mean that the iso-cost curve would touch (intersect) the highest iso-revenue curve at the Y axis.

that is purchased by specially trained buyers, who apply definite tests to the product. On the other hand, if there were zero knowledge (a case difficult to imagine) the iso-revenue curves would be parallel to the Y axis, indicating that the product should be as " shoddy " as possible,[10] as improvements will not affect the demand curve, and that expenditure should (from the private point of view) be on advertising which will favorably affect the demand curve for the product. Of course, almost all cases will fall between the two extremes.

An increase in knowledge will make the iso-revenue curves more nearly parallel to the X axis, which will make it profitable for the producer to spend a larger share of any given outlay on production, i.e. quality improvement, and a smaller share on advertisement. This will, in general, tend to increase welfare.

10 Obviously, there is some minimum positive amount that must be spent on quality—the product must " look " like what it is represented to be. Therefore the iso-revenue curves can never be parallel to the Y axis over their whole range; there is some range above the X axis where the iso-revenue curves must have a finite slope and some level below which they cannot go.

CHAPTER VII

RISK, UNCERTAINTY AND MAXIMUM WELFARE; SOCIALISM *vs.* CAPITALISM

In this chapter we shall consider a quite different type of problem that results from the absence of perfect knowledge; the problem of uncertainty. So far we have assumed that the state can determine, with certainty, whether any given reorganization will increase or decrease welfare—and to what extent. But if knowledge is not perfect, then a given reorganization may, so far as the authorities know, either increase or decrease welfare—the result is uncertain. If some of the possible outcomes of a given reorganization eventuate, welfare will be increased, but if others result, it will be diminished. To each possible outcome of the reorganization there will correspond one (algebraic) sum of compensating taxes and bounties. Thus there will be a frequency distribution of possible "welfare effects."[1] Ideally, in order to determine the appropriate policy concerning a proposed reorganization (from the welfare viewpoint), the authorities must estimate the probability of occurrence of each of its possible welfare effects, and construct an hypothetical probability distribution of welfare effects. To determine whether the probability distribution of welfare effects consequent to a given reorganization, is such as to make that reorganization desirable, we must re-analyze the preference functions of the various individuals in the community.

Hitherto, we have assumed that the level of satisfaction a given individual could attain depended solely on the money income he (and his property) could earn and the prices of the things he purchased. However, if he must make plans for future

1 For the sake of brevity we shall refer to the algebraic sum of the compensating taxes and bounties that result from a given reorganization as the "welfare effect" of that reorganization.

expenditure and is uncertain of his future money income, he may be on a higher or lower indifference surface depending upon the degree of his uncertainty about his income and his willingness to bear it.

Suppose that a given individual, *i*, believes that the income he is most likely to receive during the next year will be

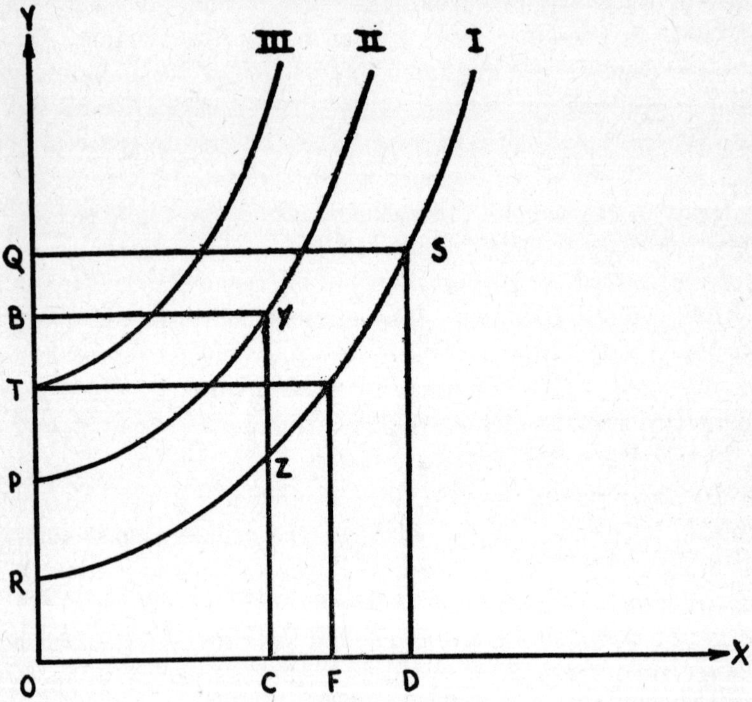

FIGURE 7

$10,000, but that he might receive an income of a different size, ranging from $5,000 to $15,000. Let us also suppose (for the sake of simplicity) that his level of satisfaction depends (with given prices of all consumer goods) solely on the mode and the range of an hypothetical probability distribution of his personal income. Given these assumptions we may construct an indifference map, for *i*, which is illustrated by figure 7.

On the Y axis of this figure we measure *i's* estimate of his "most probable income" and on the X axis his estimated range of incomes; i.e. the Y co-ordinate of each point in the XY plane measures his estimated most probable income and the X co-ordinate measures his estimated range of incomes.[2] The curves are indifference curves, each of which describes the various combinations of most probable income and range of possible incomes that yield a given level of satisfaction. The positive slopes of the indifference curves reflect our assumption that it requires an increase in his most probable income to compensate him for an increase in his uncertainty concerning the size of his actual income; i.e. to compensate him for an increase in the range of the incomes he thinks he might receive. The fact that the slopes of the curves increase with the range reflects a further assumption that he requires increasingly greater compensation in the form of an estimated most probable income in order to be willing to undertake greater uncertainty in the form of a wider range of possible incomes. These assumptions are tantamount to the usual assumption that risk and uncertainty are unpleasant and must be "paid for."

OP, in figure 7 is what Professor Lange would call the "effective income" of an individual who expects a most probable income OB with a range OC; since OP is on the Y axis, it corresponds to a most probable income with an estimated range of zero, i.e. a subjectively certain income. BP is what Lange calls the risk premium; i.e. the difference in most probable income necessary to compensate for the difference between a zero range and a range OC.

Let us assume that effective income, measured on the Y axis

2 Our figure 1 is similar to Chart 1 of Professor Oscar Lange's, "A Note on Innovations," *Review of Economic Statistics*, Feb., 1943, pp. 19-25, although his diagram is used in another connection. As Lange points out, it would be possible to construct more complicated models in which the individual's indifference map depended on more than two parameters of his imagined probability distribution of incomes, but for our purposes such elaboration is unnecessary.

of figure 7, is corrected for price changes and hence may be taken as a "reasonably" accurate indicator of the movement in the individual's level of satisfaction. In other words we shall assume (without too many qualms) that *i* will be on a higher indifference surface when his effective income increases; and on a lower one when it decreases.

Therefore, when the state is considering whether to undertake or permit a given reorganization, it must decide whether the sum of the algebraic changes in *effective* income (on account of the reorganization) for all members of the community is positive or negative. If it is positive, the reorganization will increase welfare; if it is negative, welfare will be decreased.

It must be noted that if a reorganization can conceivably reduce a community's income, this possible loss must be weighed in the balance against any increases that might eventuate from it. And if the individuals in the community are unwilling to bear the risk of loss consequent upon a given reorganization, imposing the risk upon them will reduce welfare. Therefore, if welfare is to be a maximum, opportunities must be given for hedging risks; e.g. persons must be free to make forward sales and purchases or to trade their own uncertain income (for a given period) for a guaranteed one (or guaranteed between certain limits) if they can find someone willing to make the trade.

In general, most persons are quite ignorant of future market conditions and hence are rather anxious to hedge their own risks and correspondingly averse to assuming anyone else's. Consequently risk-bearing tends to command a premium; i.e. most individuals are willing to pay to be relieved of some of their risks. Thus, from the welfare point of view, there is something to be said in behalf of the institution of specialized risk-bearing.

A community can consider itself very fortunate if it has a class of persons who are willing to assume all—or most—of its risks and uncertainties. In effect, such persons offer guarantees against income loss on account of particular reorganizations in exchange for all—or a large part—of the gains from these reorganizations. In a capitalist society, such a class of persons exists in the form of entrepreneurs. The entrepreneur utilizes resources in the production of particular commodities, the demand for which is, to a greater or lesser extent, uncertain. In addition there are risks of producing defective merchandise; of hiring inefficient workmen, etc. If the venture is successful he profits; if it fails he loses.

Let us consider a case where it is undertaken to produce a particular type of garment. Resources are diverted from some alternative use to the production of these garments. The welfare of the community will clearly be reduced on account of the reduction in output of those products that would otherwise be produced. On the other hand, welfare will (presumably) be raised on account of the output of the garments; but the extent to which it will be raised is uncertain. It might be raised more than enough to compensate for the sacrifice of the alternative products, but then again, it might not.

In a socialist society, where firms are run by salaried managers, the uncertainty involved would be born by society at large. That is, if it developed that the sale revenues of the garments were insufficient to cover their total cost, the manager would not suffer a lower income; but the loss would be taken by the state and paid out of general tax funds; i.e. born by the tax-payers. In a capitalist society, however, the entrepreneur suffers a lower income if a loss is incurred. The entrepreneur's loss of income implies that a larger share of the community's income will go to the other members of society. Thus, under capitalism, the entrepreneur protects (partially) the rest of society from loss on account of the mis-direction of resources.

However, it is not true that the loss born by the entrepreneur is always equal to the community's welfare loss from the mis-allocation of resources. To appreciate this let us imagine a " welfare gain " curve and a " welfare loss " curve for a particular commodity, X. We define the welfare gain curve as follows: corresponding to any given positive (negative) quantity (measured as abscissa) of X, X_0, the ordinate will be the sum of the compensating taxes (bounties) that could be levied (must be paid) because of an (unit) increment in the *absolute* [3] output and hence in the consumption of X, assuming that at each output of X welfare is maximized (subject of course to the limitation imposed by assuming that the output of X is given). This welfare gain curve will have a negative slope throughout, because the diminishing marginal rate of substitution between X and numeraire, for every individual, makes the compensating tax (bounty) that can be collected (must be paid) in exchange for an extra (one less) unit of X diminish as X increases. It will be easier, perhaps to conceive of the welfare gain curve if it is remembered that it is identical with the price schedule of a perfectly discriminating monopolist.

3 The reason for the term *absolute* is as follows: in comparing the welfare properties of two positions (A and B) where the outputs of X are appreciably different, the sum of the compensating taxes necessary to make everyone as well off after a movement from A to B as before, will not, in general, be equal to the negative of the compensating bounties necessary to compensate everyone for a movement from B to A. (See note 7, Chap. I.) This means that the welfare gain curve (and the welfare loss curve as well) must be constructed on the assumption of a given "starting point" to which other positions are compared. For the purpose of our argument, the starting point should be the output of X corresponding to maximum welfare and we therefore define the ordinates of the welfare gain and loss curves in terms of the sum of the compensating taxes or bounties (as the case may be) required because of the departure of the actual output of X from the optimal output by one unit more. We therefore place the origin at the output of X at which welfare is maximized from which it follows that an increment in the absolute output of X is an incremental departure from the optimal output of X.

So long as the output of X is greater than optimal, the ordinates of the welfare gain curve will represent compensating *taxes* since an increment in absolute output will be an increase in the algebraic (physical) output of X. But when the output of X is less than optimal, the ordinates of this curve will measure compensating *bounties* as an increment in the absolute output will, in this range, correspond to a *decrease* in the physical output of X. An analogous statement applies to the welfare loss curve; i. e. to the left of the optimal output, its ordinates represent compensating *taxes* and to the right, compensating *bounties*.

The welfare loss curve is defined in a manner analogous to the welfare gain curve: for any positive (negative) quantity of X, its ordinate will be the sum of the compensating bounties (taxes) that will have to be paid because of a unit increase in the absolute output of X, assuming that at each output of X, welfare is maximized (subject to the limitation imposed by the assumption that the output of X is given). The compensating bounties (taxes) will be paid to those consumers who are compelled (enabled) to consume less (more) of some other product (or products) and to those factor unit owners who are put on a lower indifference surface because of the change in employment opportunities resulting from the increase in the output of X and the decrease in the output of other products; we must, however, in computing the sum of compensating bounties (taxes), subtract the proceeds of the compensating tax (bounty) that could be levied on any factor unit owner who is placed on a higher indifference surface because of the employment opportunities created by the increase in X's output. The welfare loss curve will have a non-negative slope throughout and will for the most part be positively inclined because of 1. the diminishing marginal rate of substitution between X and the numeraire for all individuals and 2. the requirement that the curve be constructed so that welfare is as large as possible at each output of X. The latter reason implies that the sum of compensating bounties necessary to secure the factor units requisite to produce an increment in the algebraic output of X will never decrease (and probably increase) with the algebraic output of X.

The welfare gain curve is represented in figure B by the G curve; and the welfare loss curve by the L curve. The former of these curves superficially resembles a conventional demand curve and the latter a conventional supply curve; however, they are not such curves and must not be confused with them, although they do have many properties in common. The output of OB of X (where O represents zero physical output of X) at which the G and L curves intersect is the output which maximizes welfare. At this output, the welfare gain from producing an extra unit of X is just balanced by the welfare loss; at any output greater than OB, the welfare gain from reducing output by a unit would exceed the loss and conversely for outputs less than OB.

Let us assume that the economic system is so managed that, given the output of X, welfare is a maximum. Then, since the G curve is constructed on the assumption that welfare will be maximized at each output of X, it follows that corresponding to any given quantity of X, the demand price (assuming pure competition) will be equal to the ordinate of the G curve. Similarly, the supply price of a given quantity of X (assuming pure competition) will be equal to the ordinate of the L curve. Therefore if we make the above assumption (i.e. that welfare is a maximum, given the output of X) it follows that the supply and demand price of X are both equal to BD when the output of X is (at equilibrium) OB.

If, under pure competition, the entrepreneurs producing X forecast demand incorrectly and produce OC instead of OB, then the community suffers a welfare loss measured by the area DEF. But the entrepreneurs suffer a loss which must be EFJH (as the ordinate of a competitive supply curve would be CE and that of the demand curve CF) obviously greater than DEF; the loss of welfare is less than the losses of the entrepreneurs and therefore if more than the optimal amount of X is produced (given the assumptions on which the G and L curves are constructed) the members of the community (other than the entrepreneurs producing X) are benefited. If the entrepreneurs forecast incorrectly and produce less than OB, the distribution of the loss between the entrepreneurs producing X and the rest of the community can be determined by constructing an "Industry Marginal Receipts" curve, and an "Industry Marginal Expenditures" curve.

The Industry Marginal Receipts curve, MR, measures the increase that would occur in the industry's receipts if one (physical) unit more of X were sold, assuming that only one price is charged; this curve will obviously lie below the G

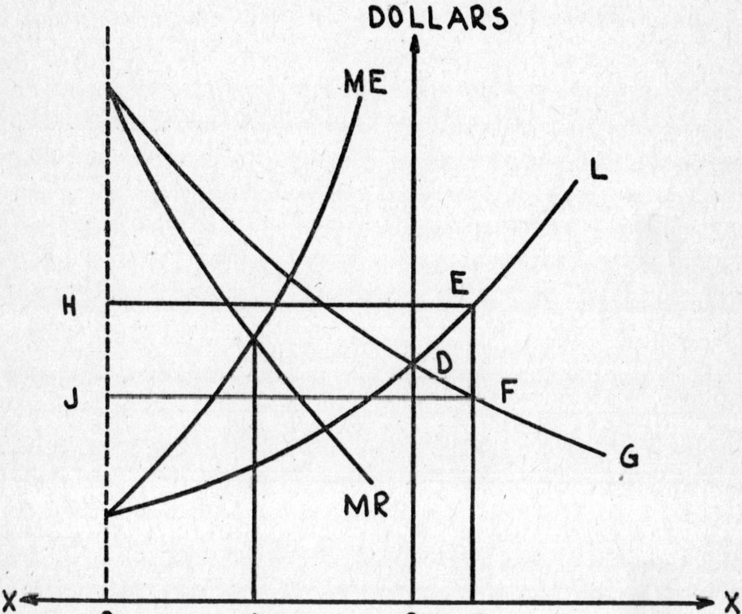

FIGURE B

curve at every point. Similarly, the Industry Marginal Expenditures curve, ME, measures the additional expenditure necessary to produce one additional unit of X on the assumption that at each output the marginal cost of every firm is equal to its average cost and that the average costs of all firms are equal; i.e. the assumption of long-run equilibrium with pure competition, counting (correctly) all rents from the viewpoint of the industry as costs to the individual firm. The sum of the profits of the entrepreneurs in the X industry will be a maximum when the industry's output is OA, the abscissa of the point where the Industry Marginal Receipts and Industry Marginal Expenditures curves intersect.

If the effect of incorrect forecasting is to place the output of X between OA and OB, the profit of the entrepreneurs will be greater than if the output were OB, but welfare will be less; i.e. the welfare loss to the rest of the community will exceed the gain to the entrepreneurs. (This illustrates the source of profit to the entrepreneurs in organizing a monopoly, and the economic justification of the objections to their doing it.) If the output should be less than OA, both the entrepreneurs producing X and the rest of the community would benefit by having output increased to OA.

It is clear therefore that individuals other than entrepreneurs are compelled to bear risk and uncertainty (as to the size of their real incomes) because of the possibility of varying outputs of X being produced, depending upon forecasts by the producers of X. If maximum welfare is to be attained either these risks should be eliminated or each consumer must be able to hedge them if he wishes. But unfortunately, the possibility of incorrect forecasting is involved in the very process of producing for a future market in which buyers exercise freedom of choice, and under present institutional arrangements there is little that can be done about giving non-entrepreneurs opportunities for hedging such risks. (We discuss below pp. 90-3 a possible method for giving consumers the opportunity for hedging such risks.)

II. Risk-bearing and Efficiency

A capitalistic society goes a long way in facilitating the assumption of risks and uncertainty by those who wish to undertake them—and thus protects others who do not wish (or are not able) to bear them. Arguments of this sort are almost stock justifications for the institutions of modern capitalism. However, a question must be raised as to whether the enterprisers are likely to be efficient in their estimation of risks. We cannot say that it is " their money and hence their business ", for as we have seen, mis-directed resources may impose a welfare loss upon persons other than their owners.

We may not take for granted, the efficiency with which private entrepreneurs, in a capitalistic society, or the state, in a socialistic society, allocate the resources at their disposal. The less efficiently they allocate them (assuming an identity of private and social objectives), the further will society depart from a position of maximum welfare. A society, no matter how great its resources and how advanced its technology, may be impoverished if it lacks the ability to direct its resources efficiently into their most socially productive uses. Capitalism's strength presumably lies in the fact that it harnesses the motive power of personal gain to the engine of resource allocation and thus assures that, under pure competition at least, the greatest efforts will be made to allocate resources in an optimal manner. Whether these efforts succeed in their objective depends upon the ability of the entrepreneurs who have control of the resources of the community. In the long run, those whose efforts succeed have their command of resources increased, while those who fail have their command of resources taken from them. This acts as a corrective to mis-allocations of resource control.

Of course, this process involves some welfare loss in that incompetent persons who manage to secure possession of resources are allowed to misuse them, and, in the cases of great fortunes, the resulting loss may not be negligible. For example, a company town, whose economic life is dependent upon the well-being of one firm, may suffer grievous economic loss through the mismanagement of the company. It is well to note, in this connection, that monoply here acts as a " facilitating agent " for welfare loss; inefficient judgment in combining resources merely dimishes profits, but does not (unless it is extreme) result in loss of resource command. Thus the existence of monopoly diminishes the truth of Capitalism's boast that it gives control of resources to those most fitted to use it.

The theory of Monopolistic Competition, as it is usually developed, shows (implicitly) how an energetic monopolist can diminish the community's welfare. But it fails to indicate, how freedom from vigorous (price or quality) competition may encourage an indolent or inefficient owner (or manager) to continue inefficient methods of production; to charge prices higher than those that maximize profits; etc. and thus diminish welfare without any monetary gain to himself.

It must be understood that restrictions on entry tend to diminish welfare not merely because they perpetuate a situation where price exceeds marginal cost, but also because they permit the continuation of inefficient techniques etc. As Scitovzsky [4] has shown, the entrepreneur does not, in general, try to maximize money profits. Rather he tries to maximize his satisfaction; and maximizing satisfaction does not imply the same behaviour as maximizing profits, except under very special conditions. Let us measure entrepreneurial activity by the number of hours [5] per week spent at work; then maximizing money profits will imply the same behavior as maximizing satisfaction only when the marginal rate of substitution between money income and time spent at leisure is infinite at all levels of income and irrespective of the number of hours per week spent at work. This condition will rarely be satisfied; in general, entrepreneurs will place considerable value on their leisure and will usually require increasingly large increments of income to compensate them for an extra hour of work as

4 T. de Scitovzsky, "A Note on the Implications of Profit Maximization," *Review of Economic Studies*, Winter, 1943, pp. 57-60).

5 This is, of course, only one dimension of effort. Intensity of effort is of co-ordinate importance, but it is not easily measured in terms of a foregone alternative and consideration of it would merely strengthen our argument.

their work week increases (income constant) or as their income increases (work week constant).

From the welfare point of view, entreprenuerial effort is just like any other kind of labor; i.e. the sixth marginal condition of maximum welfare applies also to entrepreneurial effort. Thus if welfare is to be a maximum, it may be impossible for entrepreneurs to maximize money profits.[6] If the marginal rate of substitution between leisure and income varies greatly with the entrepreneur's level of income, it may be that maximum welfare can be attained only in an economic system which uses entrepreneurial effort very intensively—and is relatively prodigal with every other factor. That is, in such an economic system, firms would be relatively large and would be run as much as possible by fixed rules (so as to economize on entrepreneurial effort) which would be changed as infrequently as possible. From the common sense point of view, the system would be managed inflexibly and inefficiently.

Under conditions of pure competition (or even monopolistic competition with freedom of entry) inefficient management is punished much more severely by loss of income, than it is when there are serious impediments to entry. Thus the marginal return to entrepreneurial effort is less under "monopoly" than under "competition" and hence there will be stronger incentives for efficiency under the latter condition than under the former.

However, a socialist society would also have difficulties in securing managerial efficiency. It must find methods of inducing strenuous efforts to allocate and combine resources correctly. A system of incentive payments to managers, not unlike giving them a share in the profits or losses made by their firm, might have to be developed. The relevant profits would have to be computed in such a way as to discourage attempts at re-

6 This need not disturb the formal argument of Chapter III, for we may assume that the entrepreneur hires hours of his own time and counts them as part of his money cost. Thus he will still be equating marginal cost to price; but he will not be maximizing his money profit.

stricting output so as to increase profits, but we cannot enter into a discussion of such problems here.

III. Some Suggestions for Increasing Entrepreneurial Efficiency

Entrepreneurs may misallocate resources by: 1. misjudging the future price at which their output can be sold and hence producing either too much or too little and/or 2. misjudging future factor prices and/or not correctly anticipating technological improvements and thus combining factors improperly. Because of these possibilities, entrepreneurs in a capitalist society require uncertainty premia in order to engage in production. If the state could diminish the range of these possibilities, it would promote a more perfect allocation of resources and, furthermore, would diminish uncertainty.

If individuals and firms were completely regimented as to their purchases, there would, of course, be no possibility of error (at least so far as future prices were concerned). To regiment society in this manner can hardly be recommended on welfare grounds; but nonetheless, freedom of choice does increase uncertainty and the difficulty of properly allocating resources. This suggests that if all purchasers could be induced to plan their purchases in advance, resources could be allocated more accurately and uncertainty reduced.

The right to change one's mind about making a purchase, i.e. having complete freedom of choice, is of *some* value to a consumer—but not necessarily infinite value. That is, a consumer might be willing to relinquish some of his freedom of choice by making advance commitments, if he were bribed sufficiently to do so. These bribes could easily take the form of special bonuses, e.g. lower prices, for advance purchases. There will be some value (in money terms) to a given firm, of a certain number of advance orders on a certain date in advance of delivery. A given firm would be willing to pay up to this amount, to consumers, in order to induce them to make this many advance commitments. If these bonuses were sufficient to induce at least the requisite number of advance commitments, welfare would be increased by having these commitments made; if the reverse were true, the gain in productive efficiency would not be sufficient to compensate "society" for the loss of freedom of choice.

A firm might be willing to pay the above-mentioned bonuses not only because of the reduction in uncertainty concerning the correct output, but also because of the greater productive efficiency made possible as a result. For, as Stigler [7] has shown, the existence of uncertainty leads to a diminution of productive efficiency, in that entrepreneurs, uncertain of future demand, make their plants adaptable to various rates of output rather than specialize them to a small range (at the limit, one) of output rates. Diagrammatically, this can be seen from figure 8, where AC_1 is the average cost curve for a plant (using "plant" to stand for all factors not continuously variable or approximately so) "more adaptable" (call it plant 1) than that for which AC_2 is the average cost curve (call it plant 2). For outputs less than OA_1 and greater than OA_2, the average cost with plant 1 will be less than it would be with plant 2, but for outputs between OA_1 and OA_2, the reverse will be the case. Which type of plant a firm will build, depends upon its expectation of the rates of output the plant will produce during its life-time. So long as adaptability can be achieved without sacrificing efficiency at any output, a rational entrepreneur will choose the most adaptable plant possible; i.e. he will always choose a plant which produces some outputs at a lower average cost and none at a higher. But, if technically possible, he may go further, depending upon his uncertainty as to future demand, and choose more adaptable plants even though this involves higher costs for some outputs.

7 G. J. Stigler, "Production and Distribution in the Short-Run," *Journal of Political Economy,* June, 1939, pp. 305-27.

This means that he may choose plant 1 rather than plant 2. Under pure competition, with uncertainty assumed to be absent, the existence of long-run equilibrium implies that plant 2 would be constructed; for price would be BP and average cost could be covered only by firms producing OB with plant 2. However, the existence of uncertainty may lead the entrepreneur to build plant 1. But if he could be guaranteed that he

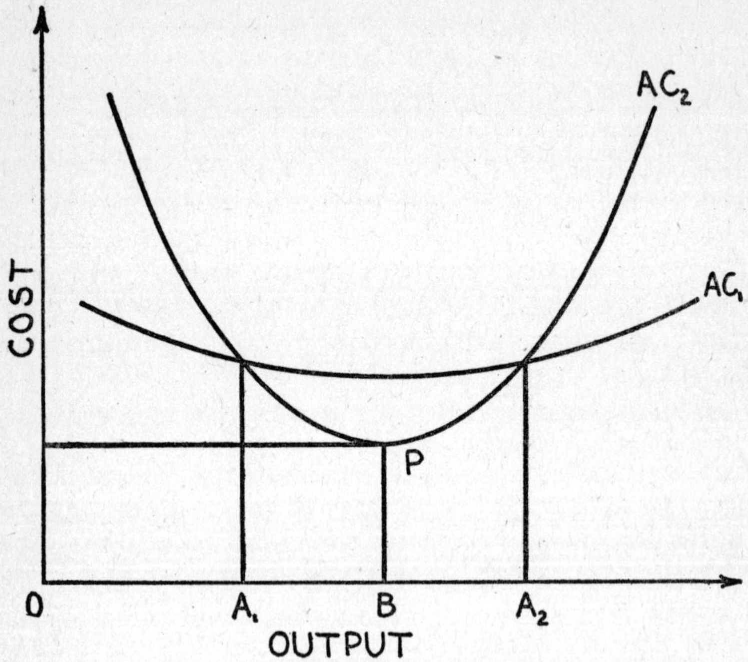

FIGURE 8

would always be maximizing his profit at an output between (say) OA_1 and OA_2 in figure 8, he would build plant 2 instead of plant 1, thereby reducing his average costs and making it possible for him to pay a compensating tax in exchange for the guarantee.

In practice, producers might offer individuals reduced prices in exchange for advance orders, i.e. the consumers would relinquish some of their freedom of consumers' choice in exchange for additional real income.[8] The amount of the price reductions would, of course, depend upon the savings in cost that could be affected and on the amounts that producers would be willing to pay to be rid of uncertainty.

There are, several difficulties in the way of adopting such a program. First, there is the obvious difficulty of determining the appropriate premium for advance orders. This could only be determined, if at all, by experimentation. Then it would be difficult for persons who are uncertain of their future incomes to make advance commitments, even though they would otherwise be willing to do so. To overcome this difficulty, society might have to guarantee an income, or at least some minimum income to each individual. We shall discuss this matter in Chapter VIII.

Lest this argument be thought entirely fanciful, let us note that entrepreneurs, on occasion, do offer lower prices for advance purchases; e.g. the difference in the price per copy of magazines and/or newspapers when they are purchased on a subscription basis and when they are purchased per issue, i.e. special terms to persons who sign long-term contracts.

It is the author's suspicion that much of the uncertainty that plagues entrepreneurs would be eliminated, if the fluctuations in National Income could be substantially eliminated. If this surmise is correct, then the likelihood of resources being misdirected on account of ignorance would be greatly diminished if National Income were stabilized.

8 Given the distribution of income at each level of community real income, a reduction in the uncertainty concerning the community's real income, will make it possible to diminish each individual's uncertainty concerning his own income. It is likely that most individuals would be willing to pay a compensating tax in order to diminish this uncertainty.

CHAPTER VIII

MAXIMUM WELFARE AND THE COMPENSATION QUESTION

I. The Analytical Implications of Non-Compensation

In our argument thus far, we have assumed that any economic reorganization which is of such a nature that the sum of the compensating taxes that could be collected on account of it exceeds the sum of the compensating bounties that must be paid (on account of it) increases welfare. However, this means that a reorganization which *actually* does leave some persons less satisfied (and others more satisfied) is said to increase welfare merely because it would be theoretically *possible* to redistribute income in such a way that everyone would be more satisfied. Consequently an economist may reject a proposed reorganization that will increase welfare, on the ground that he disapproves of its effects on distribution.

The practical effect of not compensating the victims of economic reorganizations [1] has been to concentrate public (and even scientific) attention on their distributive effects, almost to the exclusion of their impact on welfare. But the theoretical implications of non-compensation for welfare problems seem to have been quite neglected. To be specific, economists do not seem to have realized that the insecurity fostered by economic reorganizations (when no compensation is given the victims) is a social cost, and that the existence of this cost may upset the usual calculations of the welfare effect of economic reorganizations.

Let us elaborate a bit. It is obvious, if a given reorganization increases welfare, that those damaged by it will be unable to

1 Most reorganizations, both in number and importance, result from changes in tastes and techniques or the discovery of new resources, and sufferers from these changes are not compensated. And even those reorganizations resulting from state policy; e. g. reorganizations resulting from tariffs, fiscal and monetary policies etc. rarely involve compensation to their victims.

bribe (without making the bribe greater than their losses would be) those benefited into agreeing to the cancellation of the reorganization; this is merely another way of saying that the algebraic sum of the compensating taxes and bounties would be positive. However, let us suppose that there is a whole set of reorganizations, any (or all) of which may occur within a given period of time; and that all of these reorganizations would, if consummated, increase welfare, *but that no compensation will be paid to persons who may be injured by them.*

Consider a person who believes he will be damaged by some of the reorganizations but benefited by the others, and assume that he has an idea both of the range of incomes he might receive and of his most probable income, if reorganizations are allowed to occur. While in principle, reorganizations may either decrease or increase the estimated range of a given individual's income, and it is theoretically possible to find a class of reorganizations such that prohibiting all of them will increase rather than decrease the estimated range of an individual's income, such cases are quite rare. In the more interesting and frequent cases, opening the door to a given class of reorganizations will increase the range of an individual's income; particularly if the effects of different reorganizations of a given class differ widely among themselves, as is more likely to be the case the broader the class of reorganizations we consider.

Accordingly, suppose a given individual is given a choice between (1) prohibiting all reorganizations and thus preserving the status quo and (2) allowing one or more of the reorganizations of a certain class to take place. (It is assumed that 1. if reorganizations of this class are allowed, the individual will have no further control over which or how many of them actually do occur; 2. that the reorganizations would all be welfare increasing if compensation were paid to those damaged; and 3. that the class of reorganizations considered is such that the estimated range of the individual's income will be greater, unless compensation is paid, if this class of reorganizations is permitted than if it is not.)

Suppose that if a given class reorganizations were permitted, the individual's estimates of his most probable income and its range would be (in terms of figure 7) OQ and OD, respectively; and that if they were not permitted, his estimates of his most probable income and its range would be OB and OC, respectively. If these reorganizations were permitted, the individual would be at S on curve I., but if they were not, he would be at Y on curve II. In other words, the individual would be willing to pay YZ to prevent these reorganizations even though everyone of them would increase welfare, were compensation paid. This individual's fear of loss from the reorganizations so outweighs his hope of gain from them, that he would gladly relinquish some of his effective income in order to be free from the risk and uncertainty that they bring. YZ is the compensating tax that could be levied upon the individual in question as a consequence of prohibiting all reorganizations, the victims of which are not compensated. Summing, for all persons, the compensating taxes and bounties that could be levied in this fashion, we may determine whether it would increase welfare to prohibit this class of economic reorganizations. If the algebraic sum of the taxes is positive then those who would prevent these reorganizations would be able (theoretically) to " buy the votes " of those who would (otherwise) desire them and thus welfare might be increased by prohibiting these reorganizations. Whether or not welfare would be increased by prohibiting a given class of reorganizations is a very difficult matter to decide—*but there is no* a priori *reason why it should be decreased rather than increased.* If this be granted, every prescriptive proposition in economics becomes debatable.

Our argument has been stated in terms either of stopping all reorganizations of a given class or of permitting all of them. Obviously we may apply the argument without amendment to most of the broader classes of reorganizations: e.g., tariff changes; changes in productive techniques; etc. or to all possible reorganizations. It then follows, for example, that although free trade may increase welfare if compensation is paid, it may not do so in the absence of compensation. Most, if not all, of the economically important prescriptive propositions of welfare economics are subject to a similar challenge!

An extreme example may help to make this clearer; suppose five men are asked to draw cards (with no pecuniary risk) from a deck: the holders of the four high cards are to receive a thousand dollars each, and the other man is to be shot. Many, perhaps most, people would refuse to play. But if it were known that the executioner could be bribed for (say) $500, and the players agreed that the four winners were to contribute the $500, then no one could be harmed by playing and quite possibly would be benefited; in this case most people would be willing to pay in order to participate. The first case corresponds to a potentially welfare-increasing reorganization without compensation, the second case to the same reorganization with compensation. Preventing the reorganization (not permitting the game) would almost certainly not decrease welfare in the first case, but would certainly diminish it in the second.

This means that all economic policies, hitherto considered "sound", may be found (on welfare grounds) to be "unsound", unless compensation is guaranteed. This does not mean that the policies *are* unsound, but merely that they must be coupled with provision for adequate compensation. The economist, in advocating policies on welfare grounds, must assume the responsibility of urging that "adequate compensation" be given. Otherwise his entire argument for the policy may be formally incorrect.

If we may borrow the terminology of another branch of economics, the "compensation issue" may be viewed either ex post or ex ante. Viewed ex post, that is viewed *after* it is determined *which* welfare increasing reorganizations are to be made, it is always possible for the beneficiaries of the reorganizations to compensate fully those who are harmed by the reorganizations. (And it is impossible for those harmed to profit by bribing those benefited to agree to reversing the reorganizations.) But viewed ex ante; i.e. viewed before it is determined which welfare increasing reorganizations are to be made, it is possible, as we have seen, that fear of the uncompensated loss of income may be so great and so wide-spread that those, who prefer to prevent all welfare increasing reorganizations (of a given class), will be able to bribe into agreement, with profit, all those would otherwise prefer that the reorganizations take place. In short, policies which may increase welfare, viewed ex post, may reduce it, viewed ex ante.

Compensating those persons harmed by reorganizations will increase the willingness of almost every individual to have welfare increasing reorganizations undertaken.[2] The guarantee of compensation will narrow the range of income an individual will expect; raising the lower limit of the range of expected possible income in the event of being damaged by a reorganization and lowering the upper limit (because of paying the compensation taxes) in the event of being benefited. And, as we have seen, there may very well be a certain minimum amount of compensation which must be guaranteed in order that a given class of reorganizations, all of which are welfare increasing ex post, should become welfare increasing ex ante as well. But this minimum amount need not be the optimum amount of compensation that should be undertaken.

It would be well to note that all of the above arguments assume implicitly that feasible administrative procedures exist for determining the amount of compensation (positive or negative) to be given to each individual. In many cases this assumption will be far removed from reality and our argument

2 The only persons for whom this would not be true, would be those who actually like uncertainty, i. e. persons who would prefer a larger to a smaller range of incomes, given the most probable income.

must be correspondingly discounted. Furthermore, we have neglected the cost of administering the compensation process. If this is sizable it must be considered as a social cost of attaining the new organization; this cost may reverse our judgment on many reorganizations that would otherwise increase welfare.

II. The Optimum Compensation and Income Insurance

Increasing welfare by guaranteeing compensation to victims of welfare increasing (ex post) reorganizations is really a special case of what we may call "income insurance." One type of income insurance policy would guarantee its owner a specified income for a given period (say a year), in exchange for which he must surrender his actual income. If the insurance system can pay for itself; i.e. if the premia collected are equal to or greater than the amount that must be paid to the policy-holders, then it will increase welfare to create such a system. Such a system, if financed by the state, would be a system of social income insurance. Most actual systems of Unemployment Compensation Insurance guarantee a certain minimum income, in exchange for a fixed premium if the income exceeds this limit. It is obvious, however, that a very large number of income insurance schemes may be devised. Any one of them will increase welfare (viewed ex post or ex ante) provided that it can cover its costs from premia paid by voluntary policy holders. Our argument may be thought of as the "welfare case" for income insurance, of which "Unemployment Compensation Insurance" is one special example.

The welfare superiority of one insurance system over another may be determined (in the usual way) by computing, ex ante, the algebraic sum of the compensating taxes and bounties that could be collected as a result of abandoning one system and adopting the other. In this way we may conceptually determine the optimum income insurance system.

Henceforth in this book when we say that a particular reorganization is welfare increasing, we shall be speaking from the usual ex post point of view. But we shall be assuming that there is sufficient compensation for the victims of the reorganizations to nullify any objections that might be raised from the ex ante point of view.

PART II

A FRAMEWORK FOR THE THEORY OF ECONOMIC DYNAMICS

CHAPTER IX

THE CHARACTERISTICS OF DYNAMIC SYSTEMS

THE traditional theory of welfare economics has been confined to an analysis of the welfare properties of equilibrium positions. So far, our discussion of welfare economics has also proceeded within these conventional limits. However, we propose to broaden these limits and develop a more generalized theory which is applicable to processes of change, as well as to positions of equilibrium. Since, in practice, the economic system is always in process of movement, even though the movement may be toward an equilibrium position, it is all-important that our criteria of proper economic policy should be applicable to such processes. Generally, welfare economists have applied the usual "static" welfare theory to these processes without carefully considering the modifications necessary to make the transition. We shall attempt to remedy this defect.

But before we do this, it is necessary to digress in order to develop a theory of economic dynamics. Certain aspects of this theory have already become fairly well systematized, but the treatment has tended to be of a highly mathematical character, and not easily accessible to the general student of economics. Therefore in this and the next three chapters we will outline a theory of economic dynamics. Then, in Chapter XIII we shall apply it to welfare problems.

I. THE RELATION BETWEEN STATIC AND DYNAMIC SYSTEMS IN A SINGLE MARKET

Let us begin by defining *a dynamic system* [1] *as one in which*

[1] The terms static and dynamic have had a long and checkered history in economic literature. The definitions adopted here are purely arbitrary. *A static system is one in which the value taken by any variable of the system*

the value taken at any given moment of time by any variable of the system is determined partly or wholly by the values taken by that variable and/or other variables (given the parameters and the functional form of the system) at some moment or moments of time in the past.

As we have defined it, a dynamic system is one in which the variables are partly or wholly determined by the previous behavior of the economic system. In some cases when the system's functional form, parameters, and the values of its variables at some moment of time are given, the time paths of all the variables of the system are completely determined. Dynamic systems of this sort are often found in business cycle theory; three outstanding examples are the business cycle theories of Tinbergen,[2] Frisch[3] and Kalecki.[4] For example, in Kalecki's theory, the level of national income at a given moment of time t_0, is determined uniquely by the level of investment at that moment. This, in turn, is determined by the rate of investment decisions undertaken within a period of time prior to t_0, i.e. between $t_0 - \theta$ (θ is called the "gestation period"), and t_0; the amount of investment activity occurring at t_0 is assumed to depend only on the average rate of decisions between $t_0 - \theta$ and t_0, and not on their dispersion or any higher moments of the time distribution of the decisions. The rate of investment decisions at any moment of time is assumed to be determined by the volume of capital extant at that moment, and

(at any moment of time) is determined (given the parameters and functional form of the system) solely by the values taken by the other variables of the system at that moment.

2 Jan Tinbergen, "Econometric Business Cycle Research," *Review of Economic Studies*, Feb. 1940, pp. 73-90.

3 Ragner Frisch, "Propagation and Impulse Problems in Dynamic Economics," Essays in Honor of Gustav Cassel, George Allen and Unwin, London, 1933, pp. 171-205.

4 M. Kalecki, "A Macro-Dynamic Theory of Business Cycles," *Econometrica*, 1935, pp. 327-44; "A Theory of the Business Cycle," *Review of Economic Studies*, February 1937; "Essays in the Theory of Economic Fluctuations," Allen and Unwin, 1939, Chapter V.

the level of national income at that moment. Consequently, given: (1) the level of national income and the volume of capital extant at a given moment, t_0; (2) the average rate of investment decisions between $t_0 - \theta$ and t_0; (3) the parameters and form of the function relating the rate of investment decisions to the volume of capital and the level of national income; and (4) the parameters and form of the propensity-to-consume function, which relates the level of national income to the level of investment; the level of national income is determined for every moment in the future.

On the other hand, a static system is one in which the values taken by the variables at one moment of time are, given the functional form and the parameters of the system, dependent solely on the values taken by the other variables at that moment of time *and have no relationship with the value taken by any variable at any other moment.* For example, in the general equilibrium theory (as expounded by Hicks,[5] Pareto et al.) the equilibrium prices of the various commodities, the quantity of each commodity consumed by each individual, the quantity of each commodity produced by each firm etc. are determined (when the system is determinate), given the forms and parameters of the various transformation and utility functions, solely by the conditions that (1) each individual maximizes his utility; (2) that each firm maximizes its profit and (3) that the market for each commodity be cleared; i.e. that supply equal demand in each market. The equilibrium values of these variables hold only for the moment (or period) for which the functions of the system are defined, and afford no clue as to what these values may have been a moment (period) before, or will be a moment after. Any such relationship as might exist could affect the equilibrium values solely through the parameters and forms of the various functions in the system; e.g. yesterday's price can effect today's price only

5 Hicks, in "Value and Capital," deals also with dynamic systems (in the above sense) in Chapter XXIII.

by shifting today's supply and/or demand functions. But since the parameters and forms of the functions of a static system are included in its "givens," this relationship is simply not stated in the static system of either "yesterday" or "today"; e.g. an inter-relationship between the price of a product yesterday and its demand schedule today is reflected in today's "tastes" which are among the givens of today's static system.[6]

A static system, as above defined, is obviously not the same as a *stationary* system; a system *may* be statical without being stationary [7] and vice-versa. A stationary system is one in which the variables are constant through time.[8] This constancy may be due either to: 1. a repetition of identical static systems at each moment of time; or 2. a dynamic system in which the inter-temporal dependence of the variables is such as to render them constant through time. An example of the latter case would be a situation in which the output of a commodity, X, at any given moment of time, t_0, would depend on the inputs of the various factors, a, b . . . n at various moments in the past, but where the inputs of the various factors are such that the output at each moment is the same.

Viewing the matter in a slightly different way, the relations between static and dynamic systems can be expressed in terms of the adjustment period of a variable to its equilibrium position. Suppose we have a conventional situation in which the

6 "Today" and "yesterday" may refer either to "points" of time or to periods of any convenient length.

7 An example of this is given by P. A. Samuelson, "Dynamics, Statics and the Stationary State," *Review of Economic Statistics*, Feb. 1943, p. 60; the output of a crop in a given year may be a function of weather conditions in a given year (sowing constant) and hence will fluctuate from year to year. If the weather in one year is independent of that in any other, then the system will be static (as the output in one year will be independent of the output in any other), but will obviously not be stationary.

8 P. A. Samuelson, *op. cit.*, p. 59, mentions that occasionally the concept of stationariness may be generalized to include behavior periodically repetitive through time.

price of a commodity, X, is to be determined, given: 1. the demand and supply curves for the commodity, 2. pure competition and 3. that all other commodities are produced, consumed and priced at their equilibrium values at every moment in the relevant interval of time. Let the actual price, p_0, at moment of time, t_0, differ from the equilibrium price, p_e, at that moment by a quantity, Δp, and let the excess demand (demand minus supply) at that actual price, be e_0. Assume that the rate of price change is positive (negative) when excess demand is positive (negative); i.e. if demand (supply) exceeds supply (demand), the price rises (falls).

We may represent the rate of price change as a function of excess demand, as in figure 9, where the X axis represents excess demand and the Y axis, the rate of price change.[9] So far we have specified merely that when excess demand is positive (negative) the rate of price change is positive (negative). Now let us consider what the actual relationship between excess demand and the rate of price change is likely to be. If the function is negatively sloped, as curve II. is, the rate of price change is the greater, the smaller is the excess demand; if the curve were negatively sloped over the whole range, then as the excess demand became large without bound, the rate of price change would tend to approach zero. Economically, this means that if only the excess demand were sufficiently large, the price would be constant through time; i.e. if excess demand were sufficiently large, there would be no tendency for price to rise; and that the smaller the excess demand, the more rapid would be the response of the price. It also means that, although the rate of price change would be zero, if excess demand were zero, it would be "substantially" negative (positive) if excess demand were even infinitesimally positive (negative). These results, while not logically absurd, are highly unrealistic[10] and hence we may assume that the

9 For the sake of convenience we have not included the negative portions of the axes.

10 Assuming that the equilibrium position is unique.

function represented in figure 9 will not be negatively sloped. Instead it is likely to be positively sloped, like curve I., implying that the greater the excess demand, the greater will be the rate of price increase.[11]

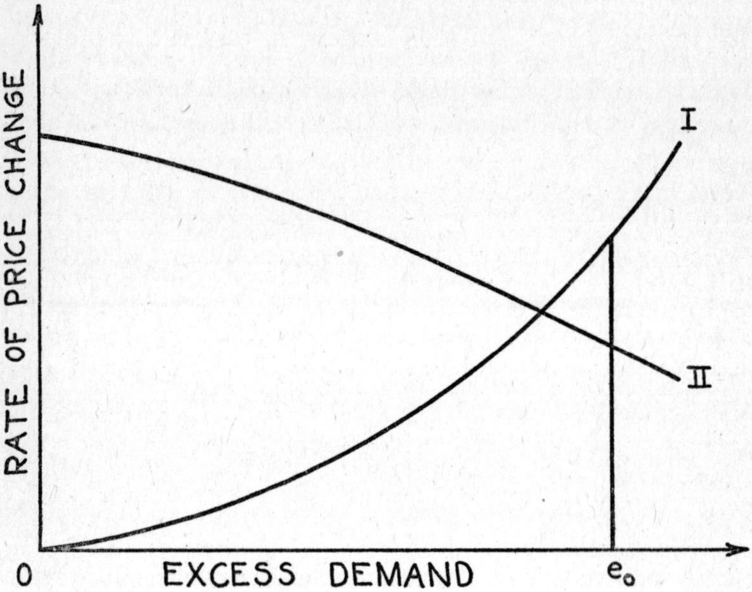

FIGURE 9

As the sensitivity of price to the existence of excess demand increases, the curve in figure 9 will shift upward and probably become flatter, in the limiting case acquiring an infinite ordinate. In other words, in the limiting case of price sensitivity, the price will fall to its equilibrium level with infinite speed whenever any excess demand (no matter how little) appears. Such extreme sensitivity of price to excess demand is very unlikely to exist in reality, but it is of considerable theoretical interest. Because this case, of instantaneous

11 The reverse of this argument applies when there is negative, instead of positive, excess demand; e. g. if there were negative excess demand, we should discuss the rate of decrease, instead of the rate of increase, of price.

adjustment of price to the existence of excess demand, is the special case in which static and dynamic systems become identical. This can be seen immediately, if we remember that in a static system, the price (the variable in this case) at any moment of time is uniquely determined by the intersection of the supply and demand curves (for the commodity in question) that exist at that moment, and bears no relationship to what it was a moment ago. But this also characterizes our dynamic system when the price is "infinitely sensitive" to the existence of excess demand, for in this case there is no relationship between the price at the present moment and a moment earlier; the existence of any amount of excess demand causes it (the price) to move with infinite speed to its new equilibrium position (where excess demand is zero); i.e. however short an interval of time we may take, the period of transition to the equilibrium price will be still shorter. Consequently, to determine the actual price at any given moment of time, all that is necessary is to determine the equilibrium price (assuming the equilibrium to be stable) at that moment of time, for the price can never differ from its equilibrium value for even a single moment. Thus it can be seen that a static system is a special, limiting case of a dynamic system (when the rate of price change in the presence of excess demand, becomes infinite).

It is also a particular aspect of a dynamic system from which we may learn its direction of movement and its "goal"; i.e. its resting point. We have not as yet examined this latter aspect of the relationship between static and dynamic systems, but we shall do so now. So far we have merely discussed the relationship between the amount of excess demand and the rate of price change. The excess demand at any moment of time is a function of the divergence of the actual from the equilibrium price at that moment, and hence the rate of price change is a function of the divergence of the actual from the equilibrium price. Hence, given the divergence of the actual from the equilibrium price at some moment of time, t_0, the excess demand at that moment is determined, and also the rate of price change at that moment. From figure 9 (assuming the relevant curve to be I) we find the rate of price change corresponding to a given amount of excess demand; if the excess demand at moment t_0, is e_0, and the divergence of the actual

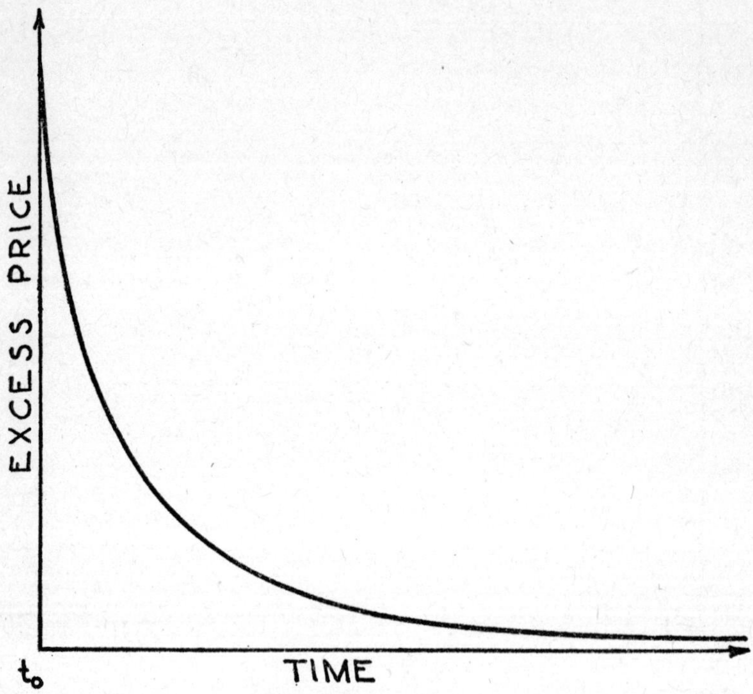

FIGURE 10

from the equilibrium price is Δp_0 (hereafter designated as the excess price at moment t_0), then the excess price at moment t_1 (t_1 being arbitrarily close to t_0), may be taken to be Δp_0 minus the rate of price change at t_0 (when excess demand is e_0) multiplied by the interval between t_1 and t_0.[12] Since the

12 The argument for this procedure is as follows: the excess price at t_1 is identically equal to the excess price at t_0 minus the change in excess price between t_0 and t_1. The change in excess price is identically equal to the

excess demand at t_1 is a function of the excess price at t_1, it, too, will decrease from t_0 to t_1, and by an amount which may be deduced from the excess demand function, given the change in price from t_0 to t_1. (This assumes, of course, that the equilibrium price is constant throughout the relevant period.) We

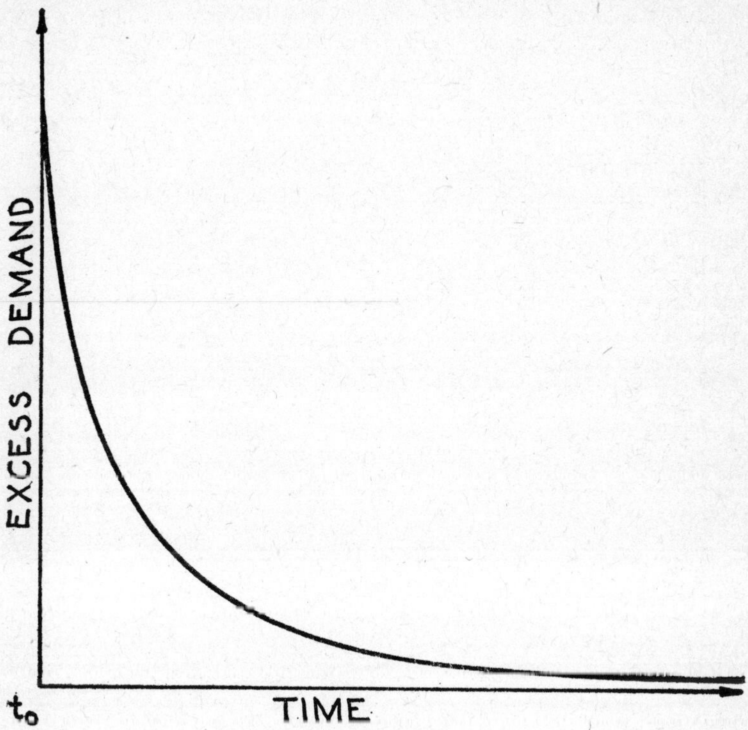

FIGURE 11

may then repeat this process for the period from t_1 to t_2 etc. Proceeding in this fashion from one moment to the next, we find excess price as a function of time—represented in figure

---

average rate of price change between t_0 and t_1, multiplied by the length of the time interval. But if t_0 and t_1 are taken sufficiently close together, the average rate of price change between t_0 and t_1 may be approximated to any desired degree by the rate of change of price at t_0. This argument assumes that the excess price function (of time) is capable of approximation by a Taylor's series.

10; the curve will be convex from below, given the assumption that the relevant curve in figure 9 is I, for (since excess demand diminishes with time) this implies that the rate of price change (and hence the total change in price in an interval of given length) becomes smaller with the passage of time. The curve in figure 11, which shows the time-path of excess demand, may be deduced from that in figure 10 for, as we have assumed, the excess demand at any moment is a function of the excess price at that moment. This curve will also be convex from below, for the greater the (absolute) change in the excess price in any period (i.e. the greater the average algebraic slope of the curve in figure 10 is between any two abscissae) the greater will be the (absolute) change in the excess demand in that period, assuming (as we do) that the excess demand curve has a negative slope throughout.

Since the curves in figures 10 and 11 approach the time axis asymptotically, the equilibrium in the X market is stable. (An equilibrium position is stable, if deviations of the variables from their equilibrium values, for whatever reason, tend to be eliminated with the passage of time.) The reader will note that we have *deduced* that the equilibrium position in this market is stable. That is, we have shown, given certain assumptions, that the existence of excess demand in a single market is eliminated with the passage of time. In doing this we have done nothing new; we have merely stated, carefully and precisely, the usual argument advanced to show that the quantity actually exchanged in a single perfect market tends to be the equilibrium quantity. In other words, there have always been implicit in " equilibrium theory ", certain aspects of a dynamic system.[13]

13 P. A. Samuelson, " The Stability of Equilibrium: Comparative Statics and Dynamics," *Econometrica*, April 1941, pp. 97-120, maintains that a dynamic theory is desirable, not only per se, but also as a pre-condition for the development of a theory of comparative statics. He argues that we cannot develop a theory of comparative statics, except as a corollary to a theory of dynamics. This means, for example, that, if the demand curve in a par-

Footnote continued

ticular market shifts to the right (given the supply curve) we cannot infer that the price in the new equilibrium position will be higher than in the old, unless we postulate that the existence of excess demand makes the rate of *price* change positive; this assumption was made by Walras and also by Hicks. But this is not postulated in Marshall's theory of long run normal price; there it is postulated that when demand (supply) price exceeds supply (demand) price, the rate of *quantity* change per unit of time is positive (negative).

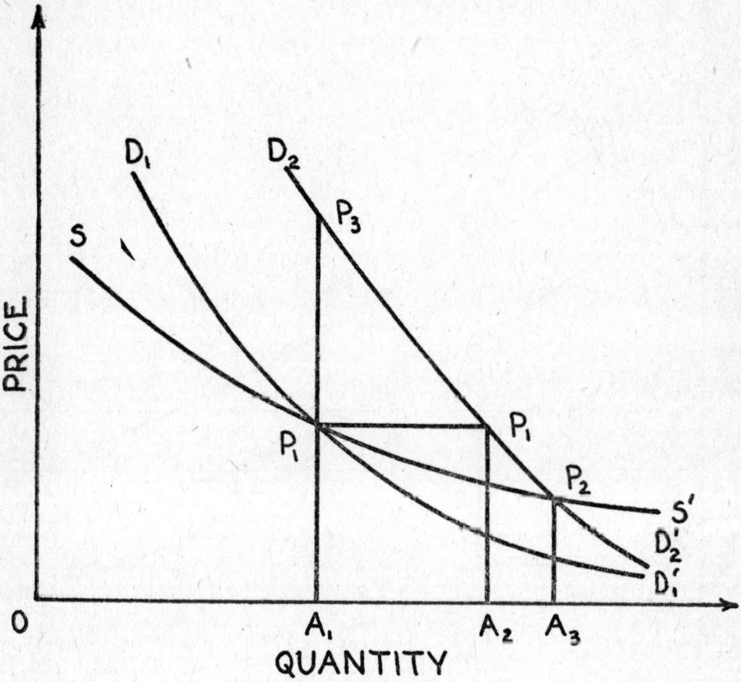

FIGURE A

On the Marshallian postulate, a shift to the right of the demand curve (given the supply curve) will always lead to an increase in the quantity produced; but the new *equilibrium* position will not *necessarily* involve a greater quantity unless the slope of the supply curve is positive. If the supply curve is negatively inclined, a shift to the right of the demand curve will increase the quantity only if the slope of the supply curve is algebraically greater than that of the demand curve. On the Walras-Hicks assumptions, a shift of the demand curve to the right will *always* lead to an increase in the price; but the new *equilibrium* position will not *necessarily* involve a higher price unless the supply curve is positively sloped; if the supply curve

Footnote continued

is negatively sloped, a shift of the demand curve to the right will necessarily lead to an increase in the *equilibrium* price only if the algebraic slope of the supply curve is less than that of the demand curve.

This is illustrated in the accompanying figures where $D_1 D_1'$ and $D_2 D_2'$ are the demand curves and SS′ is the supply curve in each figure; let (in each figure) $A_1 P_1$ represent the equilibrium price before the shift of the demand curve from $D_1 D_1'$ to $D_2 D_2'$ and OA_1, the equilibrium quantity.

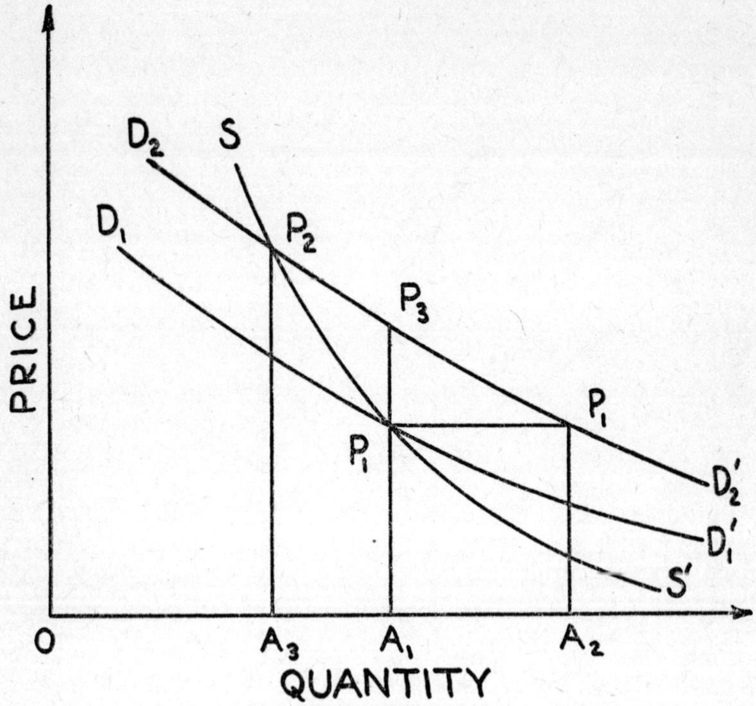

FIGURE B

In figure A, after the shift of the demand curve from $D_1 D_1'$ to $D_2 D_2'$, the amount that will be demanded at the old price will be OA_2, while the amount that will be supplied will be OA_1, and the excess demand will be $A_1 A_2$. On the Walras-Hicks assumptions, the existence of this positive excess demand will make the price change per unit of time positive (i. e. make the price rise) but the new equilibrium price is $A_3 P_2$, less than $A_1 P_1$. Hence, on the Walras-Hicks assumptions, the price moves not towards its equilibrium value, but away from it; the increase in the price leads to a decrease in demand but (since the slope of the supply curve to the quantity axis is algebraically larger than that of the demand curve) the

Footnote continued

decrease in supply is even greater and hence the excess demand increases. Therefore, on the Hicks-Walras assumptions, the situation represented in figure A is a position of unstable equilibrium. On the Marshallian assumptions, however, it is a stable position. The excess of the demand price for OA_1, after the shift of the demand curve from $D_1\ D_1'$ to $D_2\ D_2'$, over the supply price for that quantity; i. e. $A_1\ P_1$, causes the supply to increase thereby decreasing the excess demand and lowering both the supply and demand prices; but the demand price falls more than the supply price and hence the gap between the supply and demand prices is reduced as the quantity increases until, at OA_3 a position of stable equilibrium is reached. OA_3 is a position of stable equilibrium on the Marshallian assumptions, because for greater (smaller) quantities supply (demand) price will exceed demand (supply) price and hence the quantity produced per unit of time will decrease (increase).

In figure B, the situation is just reversed. Before the shift of the demand curve, the equilibrium price was $A_1\ P_1$ and the equilibrium quantity was OA_1. After the shift, the equilibrium price is $A_3\ P_2$ (greater than $A_1\ P_1$) and the equilibrium quantity is OA_3. On the Walras-Hicks assumptions, the equilibrium is stable; the shift of the demand curve creates excess demand at the price $A_1\ P_1$ causing an increase in the price. This will reduce the supply, but will reduce the demand even more, until a stable position will be reached at the quantity OA_3, with price $A_3\ P_2$. This position is stable, on the Walras-Hicks assumptions, because at outputs greater (less) than OA_3 excess demand is positive (negative) which makes the rate of price change positive (negative) which causes the supply to decrease (increase), but by less than demand, and hence the excess demand is eliminated as the output approaches OA_3. On the Marshallian assumptions, the shift in the demand curve to the right creates an excess of demand price over supply price at the output OA_1, causing an increase in the quantity which causes the output to move away from its equilibrium value, OA_3, rather than toward it. It can be seen from figure B that this is true of any position to the right of OA_3, while for any position to the left of OA_3 supply price exceeds demand price and output contracts. Hence OA_3 is not a position of stable equilibrium on Marshallian assumptions.

In short, in the situation represented in Figure A (B), a shift of the demand curve to the right will cause the equilibrium price in the new situation to be lower (higher) than in the old. But on Walras-Hicks (Marshallian) assumptions there is no tendency to reach an equilibrium position in figure A (B) and hence an analysis in terms of comparative statics of the two equilibrium positions (in either diagram) cannot enable us to predict whether the price will rise or fall. In order to do this, we must know something about the manner in which the system reacts to the existence of excess demand, i. e. about the dynamic character of the system. This point is rather obvious when we consider negatively inclined supply curves. But it is also true when we consider positively inclined supply curves, although we do not usually recognize it. For if we assumed, for instance,

We have made these dynamic aspects explicit, in order that we may discuss the welfare properties of the various paths to, and between, equilibrium positions, as well as the welfare properties of the positions themselves. Welfare economics has hitherto been concerned only with the properties of the equilibrium positions, but this preoccupation severely restricts its applicability. The economic system is constantly responding to changes in tastes, productive techniques, etc. and consequently, we may find that while one economic system, A, possesses an equilibrium position superior to that of B, the adjustment path toward B's equilibrium position is so much superior to the path toward A's, that B must be adjudged A's superior on welfare grounds. The development and application of this argument will be found below, Chapter XIII.

II. The Relation between Static and Dynamic Systems in a Multiple-Market System

So far our argument concerning dynamic systems has been

that the existence of positive excess demand caused a decline in the price per unit of time, then the existence of positive excess demand would cause the price to fall even though the supply curve were positively inclined. To be sure, such an assumption is unrealistic, but there is nothing in the static properties of the system which contradicts it and hence, in order to be able to predict the direction of the change in price resulting from a shift to the right of a demand curve (given a positively inclined supply curve), we must make implicit or explicit assumptions of a dynamic character about the system of equations describing the single market. In more complicated systems, the inter-relations between the static and dynamic aspects will increase in complexity and importance, as we shall see.

Professor Jacob Marschak ("Identity and Stability in Economics: A Survey," *Econometrica*, January 1942, pp. 61-74) argues that in some cases, static considerations may be sufficient to deduce the stability of a market system; in particular, he argues, if we could deduce market stability conditions from the principle of maximum satisfaction, then we should not need dynamic considerations to determine the system's stability. But even consumer's demand theory involves some implicit dynamics, trivial though they may be; the consumer is assumed to vary his consumption of a commodity if it differs from the satisfaction maximizing quantity, and assumptions must be made as to the nature of the adjustment path if the consumer's (and hence market) equilibrium is to be stable.

confined to a single market. Let us now consider more general cases. We have assumed, following Samuelson and Lange,[14] that the rate of change of the price of a commodity, X, at a given moment of time is a function of the excess demand for that product, at that moment. We have also assumed, so far, that the excess demand for a commodity (at any moment) is a function solely of its own price at that moment. Let us now generalize this latter assumption, and make the excess demand for a product (at any moment) a function of all the prices at that moment. Let us examine a system in which there are three commodities, X, Y and Z; Z being all other commodities. The horizontal axis in figure 12 measures the excess demand for X given the price of Y; the prices of X and Y being measured in terms of Z. The vertical axis, which measures the rate of price change of X is located on the assumption of a given price of Y. When the price of Y is held constant at its equilibrium level, p_y^0, (a level at which both X and Y markets may be in equilibrium), the excess demand for X is measured from the Y^0 axis; i.e. excess demand for X is zero at the Y^0 axis. When the price of Y is held constant at some other level, p_y^k, the price of X adjusts itself to eliminate the excess demand which exists at this price;[15] in figure 12, the excess demand for X is zero at the Y^k axis when the price of Y is constant at p_y^k; i.e. excess demand is measured from the Y^k axis on the assumption that the price is held constant at p_y^k. That is, in figure 12, the equilibrium quantity of X, given the price of Y as p_y^k, is indicated by Y^k. However, it must be understood that the

14 P. A. Samuelson, *op. cit.* and Oscar Lange, "The Theory of Price Flexibility," Cowles Commission, Chicago, 1944, Mathematical Appendix, pp. 94-9.

15 This implicitly assumes that the market for X is stable, when the price of Y is held constant. It should be noted that the system of X and Y markets may be stable without either the X or the Y market being individually stable, if the price of the other commodity is held constant.

markets for both X and Y can be in simultaneous equilibrium only if the price of Y is p_y^0.

The Y^0 curve gives the rate of price change corresponding to a given quantity of excess demand when the price is held constant at p_y^0; the Y^k curve is the same function on the assumption that the price is held constant at p_y^k. The Y^k curve

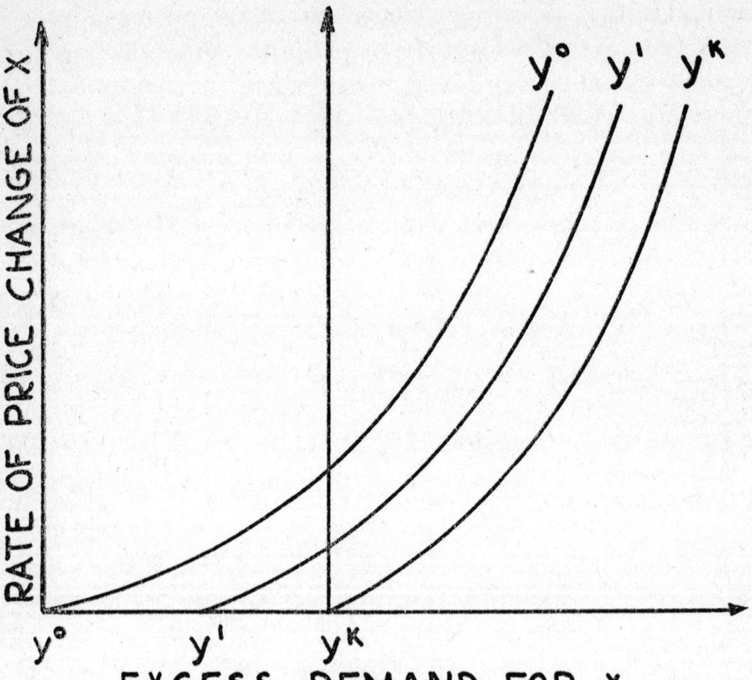

FIGURE 12

is identical with the Y^0 curve, except that it is shifted a number of units to the right equal to $Y^k - Y^0$; this is because the rate of price change of X is uniquely determined by the excess demand for X. We may, of course, erect an axis at each abscissa; i.e. given a quantity of X, there will be some price of Y, (say p_y^1) such that that quantity of X will be the equilibrium quantity. (Y^k and Y^1 were chosen in a purely arbitrary fashion.)

The behavior of the excess demand for, and excess price of, X as a function of time is given by figures 10 and 11 on the assumption that the price of Y is constant. But if the price of Y changes with time, then the time paths of the excess demand for, and the excess price of, X will be affected; if the price of Y varies, the curves in figures 10 and 11 must be redrawn. If the price of Y moves toward p_y^0 as time passes,

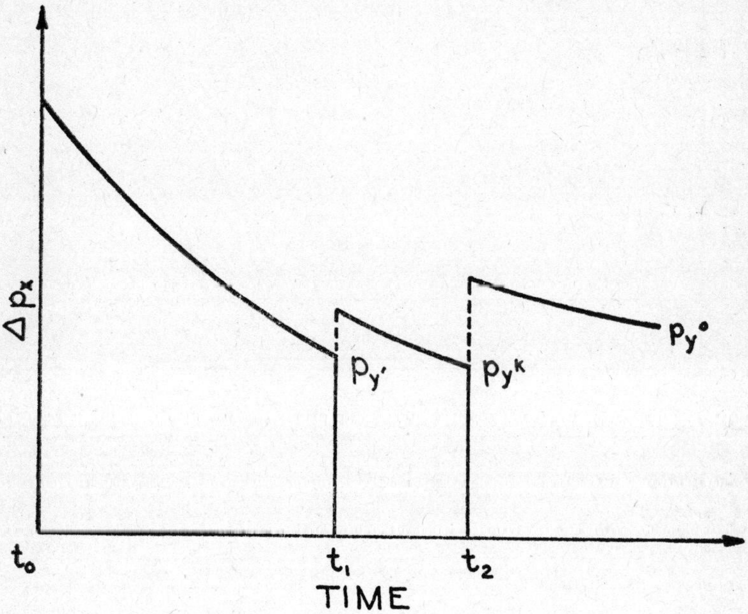

FIGURE 13

then the excess price of X will change at a different rate than it would if the price of Y were constant. The rate of change in the excess price of X is determined by the excess demand for it at that moment; the excess demand depends both on the excess price of X and the excess price of Y. (The relationship between the excess price and/or excess demand for X and time, given the price of Y, has already been explained.)

In figure 13 we draw a curve similar to that in figure 11, but which includes the effect of changes in the price of Y. The derivation of this curve assumes as given: (1) the prices of X and Y at some arbitrary moment of time, (t_0); (2) the excess demand function for X, and (3) the changes in the price of

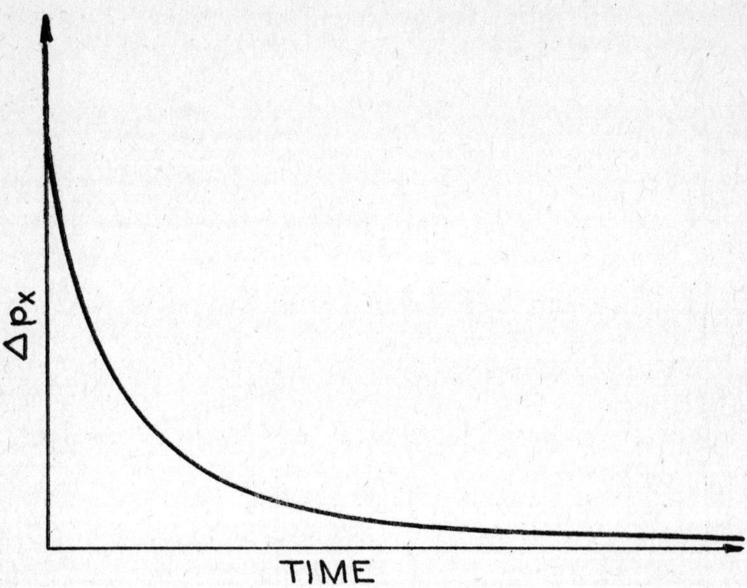

FIGURE 14

Y at moments subsequent to t_0. Assume that, at moment t_0, the price of X is p^1 and the price of Y is p_y^1. Then if the price of Y is constant at p_y^1 between t_0 and t_1, the excess price of X, between t_0 and t_1 will change in the manner explained above— in connection with figure 11. But if at t_1, the price of Y changes, the time-path of the excess price of X will also shift; as drawn in figure 13, the time path shifts upwards; i.e. the change in the price of Y at t_1 causes the excess price of X to jump at t_1. (Similarly a change in the price of Y at t_2, shifts upward the time-path of the excess price of X at t_2). The shift in the time path of the excess price of X can be determined from figure 12; suppose the price of Y shifts from p_y^k to p_y^1 at moment t_1, then the excess demand for X will increase by $Y^k - Y^1$, and the change of price of X per unit of time will be given by that particular function of excess demand for X that holds when the price of Y is p_y^1; in figure 13 this function is represented by that segment of the curve labelled p_y^1. Consequently, given the excess price of X at moment t_1, the segment of the curve relating the excess price of X to time, between t_1 and t_2 is derived in the same manner as the segment to the left of t_1; the segment to the right of t_2 is derived in the same way.

Now suppose that the price of Y changed at arbitrarily short intervals; then a curve with the same properties as the curve in figure 13 would have an infinite number, instead of three, segments, each of which would be arbitrarily short. Each of these segments would, however, be derived in the same manner as those in figure 13. Connecting these arbitrarily short segments by a continuous curve, we derive the curve in figure 14; this curve gives the excess price of X as a function of time; given a certain time pattern of changes in the price of Y.

We have seen how the excess demand for X as a function of time (figure 10) was deduced from the curve giving the excess price of X as a function of time (figure 11) with the price of Y held constant. Similarly we may deduce a curve giving the excess demand for X as a function of time from figure 14; for corresponding to the excess price of X at each moment there is a price of Y and (given the equilibrium price of Y) we obtain the excess demand for X at each moment.

So far we have assumed that the price of Y may have any time path whatsoever. But this is not proper; for just as we have determined the time path of the excess price of X, so we may determine it for the excess price of Y. By substituting Y for X (and vice-versa) in the previous argument, we may derive the excess price and demand curves (as functions of time) for Y. Therefore, the curve in figure 14 must not be drawn on the assumption that the price of Y changes in some arbitrary fashion from one moment to the next, but on the assumption that the price of Y varies in a determinate manner, described by an excess price curve, analogous to that in figure 14. But such a curve, for the excess price of Y, could be constructed only with the aid of figure 14; therefore the excess price curves for X and Y must be determined simultaneously; i.e. the curve giving the excess price of X at each moment of time (including the effects of variations in the price of Y) and the curve giving the excess price of Y at each moment of time (including the effects of variations in the price of X) must be determined simultaneously.

Given the prices of X and Y at moment t_0; their excess demand functions (depending on *both* prices); and the relationship between the excess demand and the rate of price change through time for each; the curves giving the excess prices of the two products, as functions of time, may be determined in the following way: the change in the price of X (Y) between t_0 and t_1 (t_1 being as close to t_0 as desired) is equal (to any desired degree of approximation) to the rate of change of the price of X (Y) (at the excess demand for X (Y) corresponding to the prices of *both* X *and* Y) at t_0, multiplied by the interval between t_0 and t_1.[16] At moment t_1, the excess prices of X *and* Y are equal to their values at t_0 plus or minus the changes from t_0 to t_1. Then we proceed from t_1 to t_2 just as from t_0 to t_1 and so on ad infinitum.[17] From these curves we may deduce the curves giving the excess demand for the two products as functions of time in the manner explained above.[18] Just as we have determined simultaneously, the excess price curves

16 See footnote 12.

17 Let us call these curves the excess-price time paths of X and Y, respectively.

18 Let us call these curves the excess-demand time paths of X and Y, respectively.

for commodities X and Y, we can also determine (simultaneously) the excess price (and hence demand) curves for three, four or n commodities.

III. A Comment on Substitution and Complementarity in a Dynamic System

In dealing with problems of market inter-relations, comparative static analysis classifies the market inter-relations between commodities as follows: a pair of commodities may be substitutes for each other; they may be complementary with each other; or they may be independent of each other. For a given individual, *X is said to be a substitute for (complement to) Y, if the marginal rate of substitution of Y for the numeraire is diminished (increased) when X is substituted for the numeraire in such a way that the individual is left on the same indifference surface.*[19] This refers to a given individual; the definition generalizes for all persons in the market as follows: *X is a substitute for (complement to) Y, if the sum of the amounts of numeraire that would be offered (by all individuals) in exchange for a unit of Y decreases (increases) when X is substituted for the numeraire (in the budget of each of them) in such a way as to leave each on the same indifference surface as before.*

In terms of figure 12, if p_y^k is greater than p_y^0, then X and Y are likely to be substitutes against Z; but if p_y^0 is greater than p_y^k, X and Y are probably complementary against Z (numeraire). This can be seen from the following argument: an increase in the equilibrium price of X implies an increase in its equilibrium quantity (and vice-versa), given that the supply curve is positively inclined.[20] But if the price of Y is

19 *Cf.* J. R. Hicks, *op. cit.*, p. 44.

20 In the absence of income effects, the supply curve of any commodity (or factor service) will be positively inclined (given that the firms and / or individuals furnishing the commodity and / or factor service have unique and stable equilibrium positions). On this point, see J. R. Hicks, *op. cit.*, pp. 36-37.

p_y^k, then the equilibrium quantity of X is Y^k, which is greater than Y^0. Therefore, if p_y^k is greater (less) than p_y^0, the equilibrium quantity of X increases as the price of Y increases (decreases). But as Hicks has shown, if an increase in the price of Y will lead (in the absence of income effects) to an increase (decrease) in the equilibrium price of X, then X and Y are substitutes (complements).[21] Hence (ignoring income effects), if p_y^k exceeds p_y^0, X and Y are substitutes; if p_y^0 exceeds p_y^k, they are complements. If the income effects are not negligible, then it may be that this statement is not true, but Hicks argues convincingly that it is likely that income effects will tend to cancel out—at least approximately.[22]

So far we have spoken of commodities as being substitutes or complements, in the usual static sense. This is appropriate so long as we are speaking only of equilibrium positions; but, if we are dealing with paths of movement through time, other factors must be considered. For example; on the static definition, when commodities are substitutes an increase in the price of one will lead to an increase in the demand for the other (neglecting income effects). That is, if the price of X is higher in one equilibrium position than in another, the equilibrium quantity of Y will be greater in the latter position than in the former, if X and Y are substitutes (neglecting income effects.) However in a dynamic system, inter-relations of demand and supply among sets of commodities must be defined, not only in terms of equilibrium positions, but also in terms of specified periods of time.

It may be very mis-leading to be told that X and Y are complements (against Z), when the statement is true only in the realm of comparative statics and when an increase in the price of X (at t_0) will lead to an increase in the demand for Y (at t_1). In such a case, the inter-relation between the excess demands for X and Y is such that they behave, between t_0 and

21 J. R. Hicks, *Value and Capital*, Chapter V, particularly, pp. 67-9.

22 J. R. Hicks, *op. cit.*, pp. 64-5.

t_1 as though they were substitutes instead of complements; even though they would behave as complementary commodities usually behave, if a sufficiently long period of time were considered. Such a case may occur where the commodities are (1) a certain type of machine and (2) maintenance labor for that type of machine. Suppose that the price of the machine falls; this will presumably lead (if a sufficiently long period of time is considered) to an increase in the demand for laborers to maintain the machines. But the "impact" effect will very likely be to reduce the demand for maintenance labor (at a given set of prices). For the reduced prices of the new machines will lead to a more rapid replacement of the old ones by the new ones thereby reducing temporarily the demand (at a given wage rate) for laborers to maintain the machines.

In view of such possibilities it is desirable, when asserting that a pair of commodities are substitutes or complements, to specify (1) the period of time under consideration and (2) the initial position of the system. In a strictly static system, time periods are, ex definitione, irrelevant; and, in "long run" analyses, the "relevant" time-period is implicitly defined as a period sufficiently long to allow the system to reach a position of stable equilibrium. However, in a dynamic system, a pair of commodities may be complementary against a third for reactions between t_0 and t_1, but substitutes for reactions occurring over a longer period, (say) $t_2 - t_0$. Thus specification of the time period considered is necessary.

It is also necessary to specify the initial position of the system. For if we are considering short periods of time, the relations of complementarity or substitution between commodities may easily vary depending upon how close the initial position (at t_0) is to a position of stable equilibrium. This should be sufficiently obvious to require no argument.

IV. Some Limitations of the Preceding Analysis

The argument of the preceding sections has followed the general line of dynamic analysis developed by Samuelson,[23] Lange[24] and Metzler.[25] While this work is of fundamental importance, it has certain limitations (of which these authors are well-aware) but to which it will be well to call the reader's attention.

In the first place the theory assumes that there is only one price for each commodity, at each moment of time, in a purely competitive market. Given that there is pure competition in all markets, this will be true, in *equilibrium*. But it is true *only* in equilibrium; and it does not follow that there will be only one price for each commodity apart from equilibrium. Yet the dynamic model with which we have been dealing assumes that for each moment in the process there is one single price for each commodity. It would be difficult to find many markets where this assumption would be satisfied.

Actually, what has probably happened is that in the process of generalizing static theory, the assumption of a single price for each commodity at each moment of time has proved highly convenient, and has been retained without very much scrutiny. But once attention is called to this defect, it is not easy to go farther. Possible assumptions proliferate endlessly and it might even be necessary to construct, for each market, a theory of the process by which its many dis-equilibrium prices reach an unique equilibrium value; if in fact they do. It is fairly clear, that the processes may differ greatly from one type of market to another, and thus make very general theories either useless or wrong.

Despite this difficulty we shall continue to use the model (we have been discussing) for various analytical purposes

23 P. A. Samuelson, *op. cit.*

24 O. Lange, *Price Flexibility and Employment*, Bloomington, Indiana, 1944, pp. 94-99.

25 L. A. Metzler, " Stability of Multiple Markets: The Hicks Conditions," *Econometrica*, Oct. 1945, pp. 277-92.

throughout the next few chapters. The fastidious reader may interpret "the" price existing at each moment of time as the mean of all prices actually paid in purchases of the given commodity at that moment.

Another limitation of this analysis is that we have assumed (implicitly) in our discussion (in connection with figure 12) that each market taken separately would get itself into stable equilibrium, if given sufficient time. That is, the excess price and demand time paths would either become identical with the time axis (to the right of some finite abscissa) or approach it asymptotically,[26] provided other prices were held constant. However, this assumption is unnecessarily restrictive; it is an assumption of what might be termed *perfect dynamic* stability.[27] Actually no such assumption is necessary for our analysis; it is quite enough if we assume that the system is dynamically stable, but not perfectly so. That is, we need merely assume that the system is stable when all reactions are taken into account.

But we may make quite different assumptions, which our

26 Samuelson, *op. cit.*, p. 102 defines (in effect) a system as being stable if the excess price of any commodity will become smaller than any pre-assigned number if a long enough period of time is allowed to elapse. We add the further criterion that the above statement must also hold true for excess demand. However, if the statement is true of excess price it will also be true of excess demand if the equilibrium position is unique; i. e. if excess demand (price) cannot be zero unless excess price (demand) is zero.

27 J. R. Hicks, *op. cit.*, pp. 66-7, defines a market as perfectly stable, if it is stable irrespective of how many other prices are adjusted to maintain equilibrium in their own markets—provided that the prices not so adjusted remain constant. If a system is stable, but not perfectly stable, then Hicks calls it imperfectly stable. However, the Hicksian stability conditions refer to a static system only.

Perfect dynamic stability, as we use the term, exists in a particular market, if that market is stable irrespective of the number of other prices adjusted to maintain equilibrium in their own markets *or the speeds with which they are adjusted.* Perfect dynamic stability is a stronger condition than perfect stability in the Hicks sense.

argument thus far has simply not considered. For example, if we assume 1. that when there is positive (negative) excess demand at any moment of time, the price rises (falls) with infinite speed to the level at which the excess demand is eliminated (but changes no further) and 2. that when the long-run supply price of the quantity exchanged at any moment of time t_0, is less (greater) than the market price the supply will not change for a period of time, $t_1 - t_0$, and will then increase (decrease) with infinite speed to the quantity at which its long-run supply price is equal to the market price at t_0, we get the famous "cob-web theorem."

Finally it must be emphasized that in any given situation, stability is one possible assumption. It is also possible for a system to be unstable. There may be (and I believe are) good reasons for supposing that a great many of the empirically relevant systems possess dynamic stability; but this is something that always requires empirical confirmation.

CHAPTER X

SOME IMPLICATIONS OF DYNAMIC THEORY

I. A Generalization of the Dynamic Theory

In the previous chapter, our analysis (like those of Samuelson and Lange) was restricted to a discussion of the time paths of excess demand and price for a set of commodities, on the assumption that the excess demand function for each commodity was unchanged throughout the period. If this assumption reflected the facts in an actual situation, then a time series of the prices and/or quantities of any of the commodities would merely reflect the movement toward the equilibrium level (if the system were stable). But since it is not a realistic assumption, we shall generalize our analysis, so far as possible, to take account of variations in the excess demand functions which occur during the adjustment period.

Considering the X market in abstraction, a change in the price of Y is merely one among many factors that could affect the excess price and demand time paths for X. Consequently we may re-interpret figures 13 and 14 so that they represent the time path of the excess price of X when the variations in the excess demand curve for X occur for reasons other than changes in the price of Y; and we may re-interpret the accompanying argument accordingly. The changes in the excess demand curve for X may be due to changes in productive techniques, etc. causing changes in its supply curve; and/or changes in taste, etc. causing changes in its demand curve.

If the changes in the excess price and/or demand time-path of X resulting from changes in productive techniques, etc. are such that excess price and demand tend ultimately to zero anyway, then the conclusions drawn about the behavior of a dynamic system with a given excess demand function (in the previous chapter) will also apply to a dynamic system with shifting demand and supply functions. That is, if the demand and supply functions shift in such a way that the equilibrium prices and quantities eventually become equal to constant values, then we may think of this "ultimate" equilibrium price and quantity as the ordinary equilibrium price and quantity; and the time path toward this position as the adjustment path toward the ordinary equilibrium position.

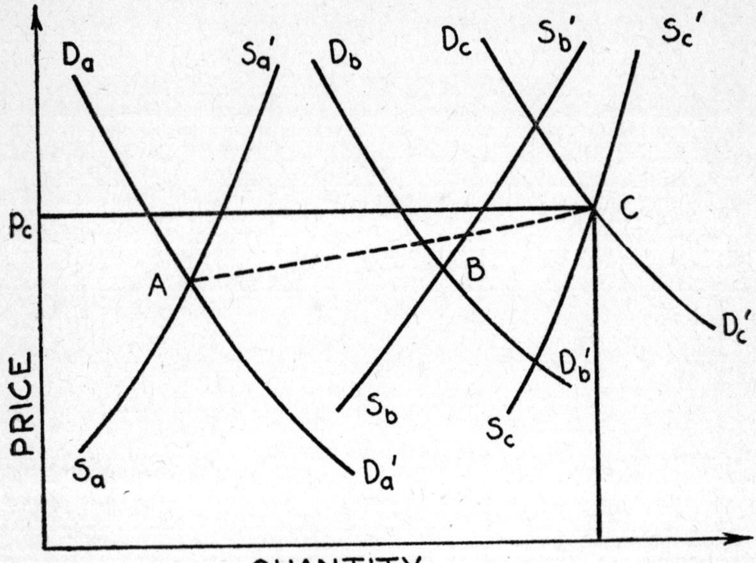

FIGURE 15

This may be explained more fully with the aid of figures 15, 16 and 17. In figure 15 we draw three sets of supply and demand curves, each set of curves existing at (in) some moment (short period) of time. These are but three of an arbitrarily large number of such curves, each existing for only a moment (or for a short period), that could be drawn. The dotted curve, AC, is the locus of the actual price-quantity points that exist between the moment, t_o, at which the system is assumed to be in equilibrium at A, and t_n when the system

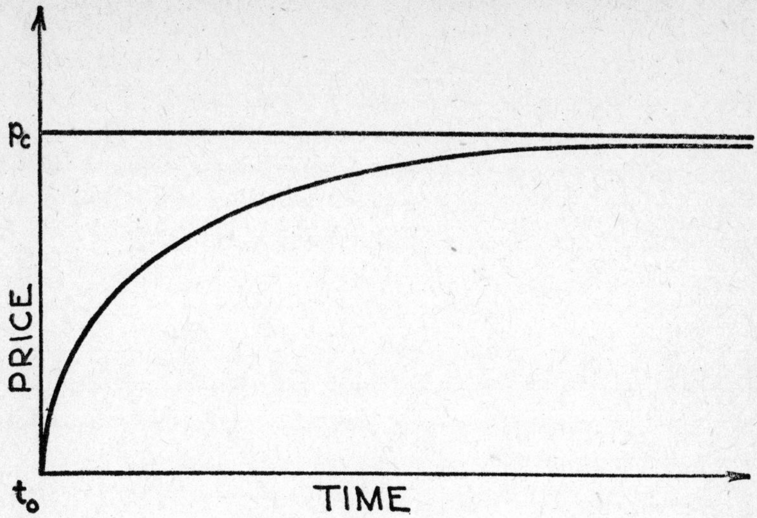

FIGURE 16

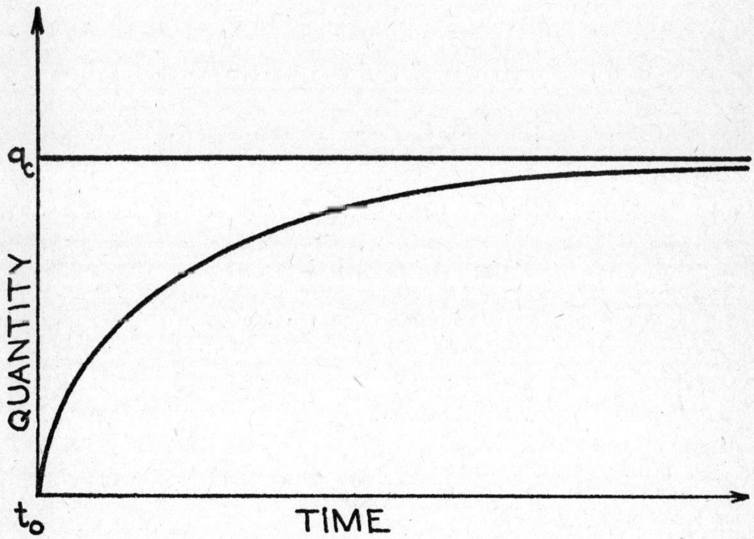

FIGURE 17

reaches its final equilibrium position at C, where it is presumed to remain thereafter. Figure 16 gives the price co-ordinates of this curve as a function of time, and Figure 17, the quantity co-ordinates as a function of time. Figures 16 and 17 show that price and quantity have time asymptotes at p_e and q_e respectively. The meaning of our argument may be understood most clearly if we realize that the price and quantity time-paths in figures 16 and 17 are the analogues of those in figures 10 and 11,[1] i.e. the time-paths are considered as approaches to the equilibrium position whose co-ordinates are the asymptotes in figures 16 and 17 and the intermediate equilibrium positions, such as B, are treated as short-run equilibrium positions in a long-run equilibrium analysis.

When the variations in the demand and supply curves over time are such that the above conditions hold; i.e. that price and quantity approach time asymptotes, the above dynamic theory (and the theory of comparative statics which is an integral part of it) may be generalized so as to explain not only the path to a given equilibrium position, but also the path of movement resulting from successive shifts of the equilibrium position. If the variations in the functions do not satisfy these conditions, at least approximately, a knowledge of the static properties of the system cannot be of much use in explaining its dynamics.

II. Long and Short-run Equilibrium

Results of some interest will emerge if, for a moment, we change our dynamic assumptions, and assume that price moves instantaneously to the level which equates demand and supply. Let us also assume that if actual demand (supply) at the current price exceeds the long-run equilibrium demand (supply) at that price, then supply (demand) per unit of time will increase, and conversely. This amounts to making excess demand, the variable, whose movement drives the system to its equilibrium position, instead of excess price which, until now, has performed this function. In other words, we are simply

1 The diagrams can be made identical by shifting the X axes in figures 16 and 17, to the ordinates of the asymptotes.

reversing the roles of excess price and excess demand; we are scrapping the Hicks-Walras, and adopting the Marshallian, assumptions.[2]

Now let us modify figure 15, so that we have only one demand curve, $D_a\ D_a'$, as in figure 18, and so that the three supply curves become $S_1\ S_1'$, $S_2\ S_2'$ and $S_L\ S_L'$. We may treat $S_L\ S_L'$ as a long-run supply curve and $S_1\ S_1'$ and $S_2\ S_2'$ as (Marshallian) short-run supply curves; $S_1\ S_1'$ constructed on the assumption that factors A, B and C are constant in quantity, and $S_2\ S_2'$ constructed on the assumption that only factor A is constant in quantity. Applying the technique previously used to determine the price and quantity time-paths (remembering that the roles of excess price and excess demand are now reversed) we may determine the price and quantity time paths (the price and quantity co-ordinates of these paths are given by the dotted curve $P_1\ P_3$ in figure 18) of the system depicted in figure 18. The variables start to move toward the equilibrium position as determined by the intersection of one short-run supply curve and the demand curve, when longer run forces begin to operate, shifting the relevant supply curve from $S_1\ S_1'$ to $S_2\ S_2'$, giving rise to a corresponding shift in the excess demand curve, and hence in the price and quantity time paths. The supply curve will continue to shift until the long-run equilibrium position is reached. The variations in excess demand per unit of time are simply the variations in supply, since demand, in the Marshallian theory, is assumed to adjust itself instantaneously to its long-run equilibrium level at the current market price.

Short-run equilibrium analysis is a useful tool only insofar as it helps to determine the shape of the price and quantity time paths. (By " shape of the time-paths " we mean the direction of their trend as well as their more detailed characteristics.) If firms vary output for some period of time on the assumption that these factors of production were constant

2 *Cf.* footnote 13 in Chapter IX.

in quantity, then a knowledge of the equilibrium position that would be attained *if* the supply curve were constructed on the assumption that these factors of production were constant in quantity, will be of help in determining the actual shapes of the quantity and price time paths. But the fact that these factors are not fixed in quantity for all time, also affects the behavior of the various firms. For example, the anticipation

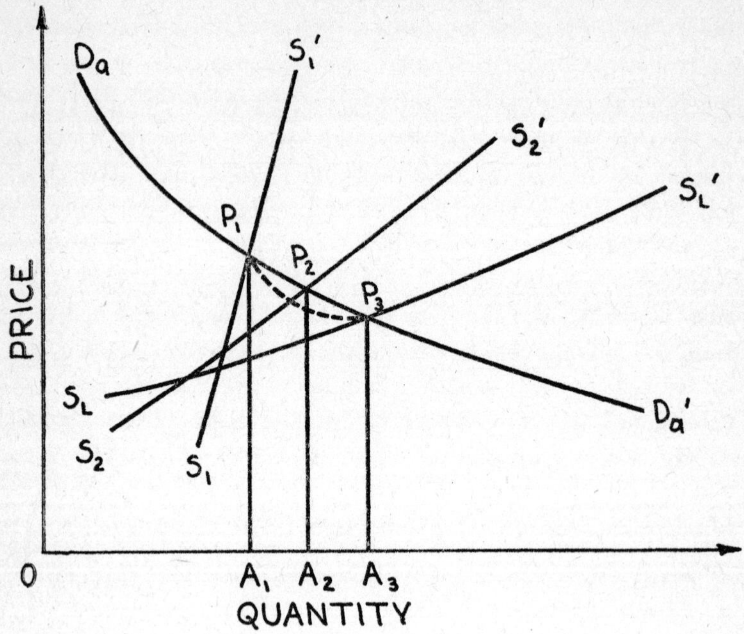

FIGURE 18

of future changes in the whole plant will inhibit many adaptations of the existing plant to increase output, and this will keep the system from attaining a position of short period equilibrium. Hence it is only rarely that an industry will *reach* a position of short period equilibrium; in practice, it will merely approach it more or less closely. (In figure 15, B, a position of short-period equilibrium is not on AC, the line of actual price-quantity points.) The more closely short-period equilibrium positions are approached, the more useful is short-period equilibrium analysis in determining the shape of the price and quantity time paths. Consequently, the utility of short-period equilibrium analysis will be the greater; 1. the longer the period of time that firms expect certain factors to be fixed in quantity; and 2. the smaller the extent to which anticipations of future changes in the quantities of these factors inhibit action on this assumption. Thus the Marshallian theory of short and long-term adjustments is merely a special case of a generalized dynamic analysis in which variations in the production functions are allowed to occur overtime.[3]

Marshall assumed that demand always adjusted itself immediately to its long-run equilibrium level at any given price. Obviously, this is not true in many cases, particularly in cases of producer's demand. Hence, we might construct a short-period equilibrium analysis of demand, the analogue of his analysis of supply. And, more generally, we might apply the analyses simultaneously, (using the concept of excess demand) in which case short-period equilibrium positions would be determined by the intersection of the relevant short-period supply and demand curves,[4] i.e. by the condition that excess "short period" demand is zero. Excess demand would approach zero asymptotically through time (in stable systems)

3 The Marshallian short-period analysis is based on the assumption that demand approaches the equilibrium level corresponding to the existing supply with infinite speed, while the supply can respond only slowly to the existence of an excess (long-run) supply price (positive or negative). Further, it assumes that supply varies discontinuously through time; that is, supply is constant during a certain time interval during which market price adjusts itself to the equilibrium level corresponding to the existing supply, given the demand curve. This price is the short-run equilibrium price.

N. Kaldor "A Classificatory Note on the Determinateness of Equilibrium," *Review of Economic Studies*, February 1934, pp. 122-36, develops a short-period equilibrium analysis which is somewhat different from the Marshallian.

4 There would be no guarantee that such positions would be reached or even approached closely.

as before, but instead of excess demand being affected solely by variations in supply, it would also be affected by variations in demand.

III. The Equilibrium of an Industry

One of the most criticized aspects of Marshall's "Principles" is his treatment of the supply curve of an industry. Marshall argued that the industry's long-run supply curve may be negatively inclined due to the action of "increasing returns." [5] This proposition is not denied; but he further maintained that competition [6] could co-exist with a negatively inclined supply curve and it is this contention that has provoked a storm of controversy. A negatively inclined supply curve not only raises questions as to the stability of the industry's equilibrium, as we have already seen,[7] but it also raises questions as to the stability of the equilibrium of every firm within the industry. For if supply price (and hence unit cost) falls as output increases, then it would seem that (at least some) firms could increase their profits by expanding their output and reducing average cost while (assuming pure competition) leaving price unaffected. However, a negatively inclined supply curve may be reconciled with the stability of the firm's equilibrium under pure competition if the economies of scale are *external to* the firm. But, as Sraffa has shown,[8] such a reconciliation is not altogether satisfactory.

5 Alfred Marshall, "Principles of Economics," Macmillan and Co., 8th edition, 1920, Book V, Chapter XII.

6 As Marshall introduces marketing difficulties into the picture, it is not clear that he was thinking of pure competition. However, it is usually agreed that Marshall did have more or less "pure" competition in mind in this connection.

7 See footnote 13 of the preceding chapter. Marshall was also well aware of this; see *op. cit.* Appendix H, pp. 805-9.

8 *Cf.* Pierro Sraffa, "The Laws of Cost under Competitive Conditions," *Economic Journal*, pp. 535-50, Dec. 1926.

In fact most modern theorists simply consider long-run falling supply curves for an industry as unimportant intellectual curiosa. They, following Sraffa, conclude either that the long-run supply curve of the industry is positively inclined (at least in the vicinity of the equilibrium position) or that the industry becomes a monopoly.[9] This argument is, of course, valid if we are dealing with a static system. However, Marshall explicitly denied that he was doing this,[10] and while his own argument may have not been altogether clear (mainly, I suspect, because of a confusion of static and dynamic considerations), it is possible to devise a satisfactory dynamic argument in defense of his position.

Let us begin by assuming that the long-run optimum size of the firm is at least as large as that of the whole industry; i.e. that the firm's minimum long-run average cost point will be reached at an output as great or greater than the industry's long-run equilibrium output. But let us also assume that the greater the rate of *increase* of output at a given moment of time, t_1, the greater will be the average and marginal cost of producing any given output at that moment. It follows from this that, marginal and average cost *may*[11] be increasing with the rate of output at t_1, given the rate of output at t_0.[12] This will be the more likely, the closer t_1 is to t_0.

9 A negatively inclined supply curve may, of course, also be compatible with long-run stable equilibrium of the industry if there are economies of scale external to the firm. But we shall ignore this possibility as we wish to take "the bull by the horns" and defend Marshall's position without having recourse to this possibility.

10 A. Marshall, *op. cit.*

11 We emphasize that this *may* occur; of course, we cannot prove that it will. It is desired only to indicate the possibility of its occurrence.

12 In effect we are saying that those internal diseconomies of scale that are usually cited as limiting the size of the firm; e. g. diseconomies of large-scale management; the "Principle of Increasing Risk," etc., may be unimportant or even inoperative in the long run, but are very important in the short. For example, an expansion in the scale of a firm's operations may not

Granted this possibility, if the excess of the industry's long-run equilibrium output over its actual output is very large, it may be some time before the various firms will expand sufficiently in size to compel such a reduction in their numbers as to eliminate pure competition. If the demand curve for the industry's product is shifting to the right through time this will, of course, delay the attainment of long-run equilibrium and make it possible for pure competition to exist indefinitely.

In short, each firm in the industry will have a profit maximizing output at each moment of time; this output, however, will increase from one moment to the next. A firm will make less than its maximum possible profits if it expands either at too rapid or at too slow a rate. The optimum rate of expansion at any moment is given by the usual condition (for pure competition) that the marginal cost of producing a given rate of output at that moment is equal to the price of the product; but the shape and position of the cost function will depend upon the previous output rate as well as upon the state of productive techniques and factor prices.[13] Provided the industry's demand curve continued to shift to the right, this state of affairs might continue indefinitely.

It is not our intention to prove that situations such as this actually occur. We desire only to show that a determinate size of the firm and output of the industry for any given moment of time is logically compatible with pure competition even thought the industry's long-run supply curve is negatively inclined. Our purpose is not so much to defend Marshall's position on this matter as to indicate concretely how a careful

---

involve any diseconomies (and perhaps the reverse) provided the management has time to adapt itself. But it will involve much waste and inefficiency, if the management does not have sufficient time to reorganize the productive arrangements so as to obtain the maximum output that can be derived from a given quantity of factor units of various types.

13 It will also depend upon expectations of future changes in output, etc.

disentangling of static from dynamic factors can throw some light upon a mooted theoretical question.

Thus, although eventually there would be only one firm [14] in the industry which would have an equilibrium output in excess of zero (all other firms being forced out of business) still over a certain time interval (which might be very long in practice) a very large number of firms might have a positive equilibrium output at each moment of time. Plotted against time, each firm would have an equilibrium output time path. If the firm's actual output deviated, at any moment, from this path, the difference would be the (positive or negative) excess output at that moment. And forces (the desire for greater profits) would tend to bring the actual output back to the equilibrium output; i.e. make the actual and equilibrium output time paths identical. Thus a "moving equilibrium" would exist—and stability would consist of a tendency to return to a rate of change of output rather than to a given rate.

14 Which firm would be the survivor and the exact pattern of events that occur once it became unprofitable for the current number of firms to remain in the industry is another question; and one which we shall not undertake to answer here.

CHAPTER XI

MONOPOLISTIC COMPETITION IN A DYNAMIC SETTING

In Chapter IX we outlined the theory of dynamic price determination as it applies to commodities produced under pure competition. Now, we shall, in the first section of this chapter briefly elucidate the theory with reference to commodities produced under conditions of monopolistic competition. In the second section, we shall scrutinize carefully the concepts of Pure and Monopolistic Competition in the light of dynamic theory.

I. Dynamic Aspects of Monopoly Pricing

Let us commence our discussion by giving a reformulation of the duopoly problem; in the static formulation reaction curves are constructed as shown in figure 19.[1] The reaction curve which intersects the horizontal axis at X_1 gives the equilibrium output of firm 1 given the output of firm 2; the reaction curve which intersects the horizontal axis at X_2, gives the equilibrium output of firm 2, given the output of firm 1. The point E, where the curves intersect is an equilibrium position, since neither firm would vary its output once both firms reached this position. In order to analyze the stability conditions of the system, let us introduce dynamic considerations; E will be a position of stable equilibrium if the rate of change of output of both firms has the same sign as the excess of the equilibrium over the actual output. For example, suppose that firm 2 produces OC_1 and firm 1 produces $C_1 D_1$; then firm 2 would have to produce OC_2 in order to be in equilibrium. But OC_2—OC_1 is positive and, assuming the rate of change of output is of the same sign, output will increase through

1 *Cf.* for example, R. G. D. Allen, *Mathematical Analysis for Economists*, Macmillan, 1938, pp. 200-4, 345-7.

time and will move from OC_1 toward OC_2. Taking OC_1 as the initial output of firm 2, and C_1D_1 as the output of firm 1, at t_0, we may construct a time-path of the output of firm 2.

Given the initial situation, firm 2's equilibrium output is OC_2 and hence, given our assumption, output per unit of time

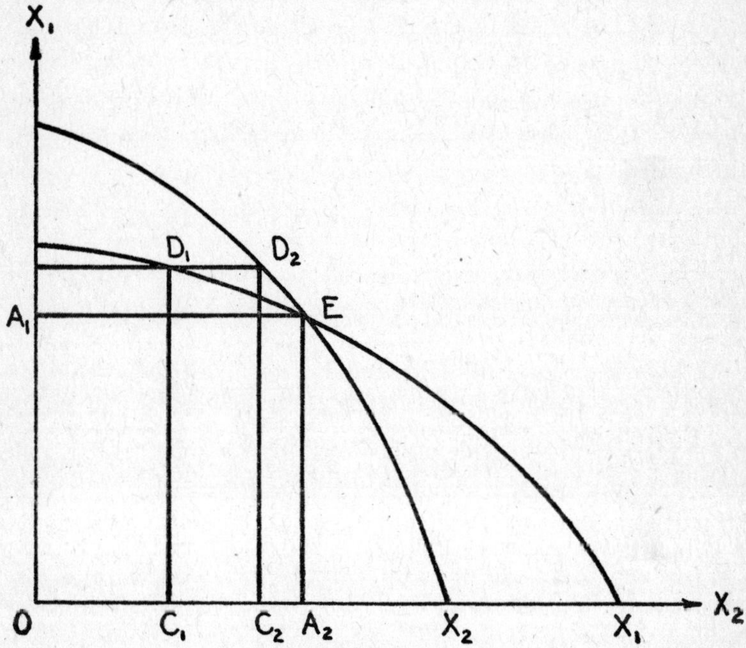

FIGURE 19

will increase. If firm 1's output remained constant at C_1D_1, then 2's output would continue to increase until it reached OC_2. However, as the output of firm 2 increases, the output of firm 1 will also change—it will decrease. For all outputs of firm 2 larger than OC_1, the equilibrium output of firm 1 is less than C_1D_1, as can be seen from the reaction curve, X_1; when firm 2's output is OC_2 the equilibrium output of firm 1 is less than C_2 D_2. Hence, assuming that firm 1 reacts to changes in firm 2's output, the time path of the output of firm

2 cannot be constructed on the assumption that firm 1's output is constant at C_1 D_1. Instead, we must construct the output time-paths of firm 1 and firm 2 simultaneously, just as we constructed excess-price time paths for two related commodities. If we assume that the greater the difference between the actual and the equilibrium output of one firm, given the output of the other, the greater will be the rate of change of output (by the former firm), then the output of both firms will approach their equilibrium values, at E, through time, asymptotically.

This argument is entirely analogous to that advanced in the process of deriving the excess price and quantity time-paths for two related commodities. Here, too, it must be understood that our argument cannot *prove* that a given duopoly situation has a stable solution; we must make certain assumptions about the time paths in order to get a stable solution.

The above argument assumed implicitly that both firms responded to each other only by output variations, and allowed prices to fall to those levels at which the outputs could be sold. However, we might make the reverse assumption and assume that the firms respond only by changing prices and selling what outputs they can at those prices. In this case, we can apply the previous analysis, merely substituting "prices charged" for "outputs produced." It is, of course, possible to have an unstable equilibrium position if the firms act by varying prices, while the equilibrium would be stable if they reacted by varying outputs — or vice-versa. This is exactly analogous to the problem of stable equilibrium with a negatively inclined supply curve which was analyzed above.[2] We may also have situations in which one firm is a price adjuster and the other an output adjuster; the reader may apply the above analysis to this case as an exercise, but the problem is of no particular interest.

It may be that the duopolists will attempt to anticipate each other's responses to their own behavior (and perhaps even

2 *Cf.* footnote 13, Chapter IX.

anticipate each other's anticipations, etc.). These anticipated responses, known as conjectural variations, are important determinants of the shapes of the reaction curves. If the conjectural variations of each duopolist, about the behavior of the other, are consistent with the other's actual behavior, then the shapes of the output and price time paths are implicitly determined. However, if the conjectures of one duopolist, A, about the other's, B's, behavior are inconsistent with B's actual behavior, then A's conjectural variations, and consequently his output and price time paths will be affected. Such changes may be treated as changes in the parameters of A's imagined demand function, which affect both his quantity and price time paths just as the parametric changes in the excess demand function affected the time path of excess demand in Chapter X. Changes in A's conjectural variations might very well cause B's conjectural variations to change also, which in turn would cause changes in A's conjectural variations etc. This makes it necessary to determine A's and B's quantity or price time paths simultaneously (just as the excess price time paths for two related commodities had to be determined simultaneously). If they approach limiting values with the passage of time, then these limiting values will be positions of stable equilibrium. It is not proposed to analyze the conditions under which such limiting values are approached; for there is a considerable literature on the subject [3] where these conditions are analyzed in detail. Although these analyses are not usually cast [4] in dynamic terms, their dynamic content

3 *Cf.* J. R. Hicks, "The Theory of Monopoly," *Econometrica*, Jan. 1935, pp. 1-20 and G. J. Stigler, "Some Notes on the Theory of Duopoly," *Journal of Political Economy*, 1940, pp. 521 *et seq.*

4 A. Smithies gives a mathematical analysis of the dynamic stability conditions for duopoly in the *Quarterly Journal of Economics*, November 1940, pp. 95-115 and extends the analysis to the case of n competitors in "The Stability of Competitive Equilibrium," *Econometrica*, July-October, 1942, pp. 258-74. Our literary argument is essentially an application of the Samuelson-Lange technique to the duopoly problem, but Smithies' technique is not essentially different, as he admits; *cf.* ft. 8, p. 266 of the second reference.

is quite clear, and it is unlikely that the conclusions reached would require major amendment in order to be put on a dynamic basis.

The previous argument can be generalized to cover the cases of triopoly, oligopoly and ultimately, pure competition. Adding firms to the analysis is a process analytically identical to adding additional commodities in our analysis of multiple market situations. The stability conditions for these multiple firm situations imply that eventually the outputs or prices (as the case may be) of these firms must approach their equilibrium values; there is, of course, no guarantee that any given system is stable.[5] In the limiting case, pure competition, the reaction curve of any firm with respect to the behavior of any other firm, (price or output as the case may be) would be a straight line parallel to the axis referring to the other firm's behavior, indicating that the price charged or output produced is independent of the price (output) of any other firm.[6] However, the absence of slope in the reaction curves is not a criter-

5 Smithies, *op. cit.*, investigates these stability conditions for firms with linear cost and demand functions.

6 Diagrammatically, the reaction curves under pure competition would be as in figure A; the equilibrium position is at E.

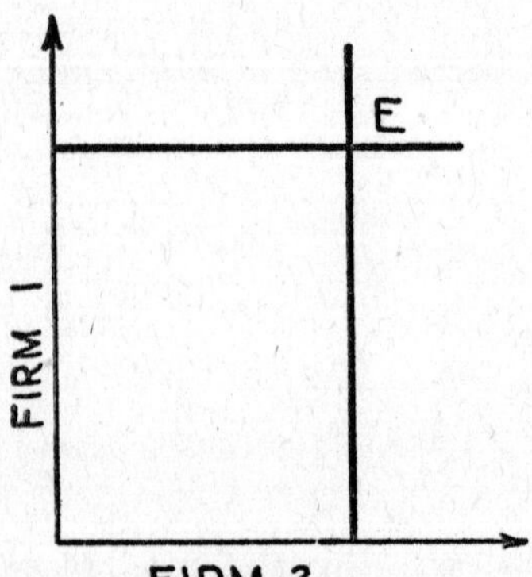

FIGURE A

ion of pure competition; in Chamberlin's "large group" case, where the competitors produce differentiated products, the reaction curves would also have zero slopes. That is, under these conditions, no one firm will be sufficiently affected by the variation of any one competitor's output or price, to make it profitable for it to respond by varying either its price or output.[7]

II. The Concepts of Pure and Monopolistic Competition in a Dynamic Setting

Recent theorists of monopolistic competition, with the notable exception of E. A. G. Robinson,[8] have tended to treat the demand and cost functions of the individual firms as being constant through time. By doing this they obscure certain of the forces that tend, with the passage of time, to diminish the importance of the monopoly elements in a market. For example, Schumpeter's innovator is a monopolist; his definitive characteristic in his uniqueness [9] and hence he must be temporarily, at least, a monopolist. If he is successful, he will be followed by a swarm of imitators (assuming freedom of entry) who will reduce him to the status of a pure competitor; or, if there is product differentiation, to the status of a member a large group. That is, with the passage of time, the innova-

7 Pure competition is distinguishable from Chamberlin's "large group" case in terms of the reaction of the firm's sales to a change in its own price. Under pure competition the change of sales with respect to a change of price is infinite, whereas under any form of monopolistic competition, it will be finite. The dynamic question, which we shall discuss in the next section, is how long a time interval must elapse before the difference between pure and monopolistic competitors, in response to a price change, becomes either apparent or important.

8 E. A. G. Robinson, *Monopoly*, Nisbet and Cambridge University Press, 1941.

9 Of course, it is conceivable that two or even several entrepreneurs might make the same innovation simultaneously, in which cases we might have temporary duopoly or oligopoly. However, we shall omit consideration of such cases.

tor's reaction curve tends to become horizontal (in the sense mentioned above). The shifts in the demand curves, cost curves and conjectural variations that are the concomitants of this process of "innovation, imitation and elimination" are reflected in the price and output time paths of the various firms. Analysis of these paths is necessary if we are to understand a theory such as Schumpeter's; the comparison of successive instantaneous equilibrium positions will not do as a substitute, for there is no a priori reason for supposing these equilibria to be reached, and even if there were, it might be essential to know the time consumed in passing from one position to the other.

As Robinson [10] points out, most monopolies result from *temporary* advantages (of one kind or another) possessed by certain producers, which are eliminated with the passage of time. That is, freedom of entry becomes "more perfect" [11] with the passage of time. While with respect to some advantages this is not true; e.g. patents, restrictive agreements, cartels, etc., it is an important factor, worthy of consideration in any theory of monopoly or monopolistic competition. Of course, this sort of phenomenon is not completely overlooked in current theory; it is handled by distinguishing between short and long run equilibria. But this approach will not suffice in many cases; if we are interested in the time path of the variables (and for many problems we are) a knowledge of the equilibrium positions can at best give the limit toward which the variables tend, and, under certain conditions, various way-points which they will approach in passing (these way-points are short-run equilibrium positions). But the analysis throws no light on the speed with which the variables

10 E. A. G. Robinson, *op. cit.*

11 By perfect "freedom of entry" we mean a situation where any entrepreneur can produce a product identical with that produced by any other and at the same total cost for any output. This, of course, implies that there cannot be *perfect* freedom of entry so long as there is product differentiation.

move (and this information is very important for many problems of price analysis); if the parameters of the cost and demand curves change through time in such a way that the time path of the relevant variable (price or output, as the case may be) does not approach a limit, then equilbrium analysis can provide no information whatever.

The above remarks are not intended as a cavil at the painstaking and path-breaking work done in the field of monopolistic competition within the last decade. Most of the authors in the field would (I think) be very likely to agree with most of what has been said. However, there has been a tendency to ignore "dynamic" problems in this area; mainly because the techniques available do not enable much to be said about them in a general way. It is, of course, far easier to exhort others to create a dynamic theory than to do it oneself, and it is not my intention to join the numerous band of "side-line" critics of current price theory. However, the tendency to ignore dynamic problems (or perhaps to relegate them to the background) has had certain unfortunate theoretical consequences that are not always appreciated.

One of these is that the usual definition of pure competition is formally invalid for all positions, except those of equilibrium. Pure competition is defined, almost universally, as a situation in which every firm in the industry has (1) an infinitely elastic demand curve for its own output and (2) infinitely elastic supply curves (to itself) of all factors of production that it uses. Triffin,[12] however, has criticized this definition on the ground that it mistakes "symptom" for "disease"; i.e. pure competition requires that the demand curve of the firm be infinitely elastic, but the converse statement does not hold. He gives, as an example, (to show the inadequacy of the usual definition) the situation where an *isolated* seller is confronted, for the relevant range of outputs, with an infinitely elastic demand curve. This demand curve

12 Triffin, *op. cit.*, pp. 137-41.

might exist for various reasons; e.g. peculiarly shaped indifference maps of consumers; belief in a "just price" for the article and a refusal to pay more under any conditions, etc. But it is not essential that we find examples to illustrate the case—it is sufficient if we can merely conceive of it and, since we can, the customary definition is unsatisfactory. Triffin solves the problem by defining pure competition as a relationship between competitors which exists when 1. the cross elasticity of demand for the product (factor) of by one of the competing firms with respect to the price charged (paid) by any one of the others is infinite, and 2. the cross elasticity of the price charged by any one firm with respect to the output of any one of the others is zero. When these conditions are satisfied, the demand curve for an individual firm is infinitely elastic; but this fact is not used as a definitive characteristic of pure competition.

Although Triffin has shown that a firm may not be a pure competitor, and still have an infinitely elastic demand curve, he has not shown the converse, which also happens to be true; i.e. a firm may not have an infinitely elastic demand curve and still be a pure competitor. This proposition contradicts the general belief that pure competitors must have infinitely elastic demand curves. Triffin's definition of pure competition would exclude this possibility, but the usual one, e.g., Chamberlin's,[13] would not.

So long as the definition of pure competition that we adopt does not imply that all buyers and sellers have complete know-

13 E. H. Chamberlin, "The Theory of Monopolistic Competition," 3rd edition, Harvard Press, 1938, p. 7; "A sole prerequisite to pure competition is indicated—that no one have any degree of such control (over price)—there must be a large number of buyers and sellers so that the influence of any one or of several in combination is negligible—control over price is completely eliminated only when all producers are producing the identical goods and selling it in the identical market—if the produce of any one seller is slightly different from those of others, he has a degree of control over the price of his own variety, whereas under pure competition he can have no control over the price of anything."

ledge of each other's trading schedules (and few do), our proposition can be proved without difficulty. Suppose one seller charges a price which is higher than that charged by another who is selling an identical product; if there is pure competition and rational behavior, the usual theory would lead us to expect that nothing would be purchased from the higher priced seller. But if a consumer, not knowing the market, came to the higher priced seller first, there is nothing in the concept of pure competition, or of rational behavior, to exclude the possibility of his dealing with this seller. This difficulty was recognized by Edgeworth, who tried to circumvent it by permitting re-contracting; i.e. he regarded all offers to buy or sell as tentative " until the market " has hit upon a set of agreements which cannot be varied with advantage to any of the contracting parties.[14] However, recontracting of this sort is not permitted in most markets; and if it were, the only exchanges that could take place would occur in positions of stable equilibrium. This point was also recognized by Chamberlin, who devoted several pages to a discussion of the variations of prices through time in their path toward, or about, their equilibrium levels.[15] However, he apparently did not see the implications of it for the concept of pure competition.

A pure competitor who set his price above that of other competitors might, in the course of time, make some sales to ignorant and/or hasty buyers. These sales, would, of course, be disequilibrium sales, but we cannot exclude the possibility of their occurring without including in the concept of *pure* competition, elements of *perfection* which Chamberlin (and his followers) desire specifically to exclude. In short, there may be a demand curve for a pure competitor which is not infinitely elastic; the demand curve would very likely be thought by the seller to be negatively inclined, as the greater the difference

14 F. Y. Edgeworth, " Papers Relating to Political Economy," vol. II, p. 314.

15 E. H. Chamberlin, *op. cit.*, pp. 25-9.

between his price and the "general run" of prices, the greater would be the likelihood that a prospective buyer would recognize that the price is above the "competitive" level and would refuse to buy; and/or that the hasty buyer would be unwilling to pay the extra price in order to save time.

If the seller has some particular advantage, e.g. of service, location, etc. which enables him to get more sales than a competitor could at the same price, then there is an element of product differentiation which precludes pure competition. But even if all sellers were identical in every respect, one or more might raise his price above the purely competitive equilibrium level without losing all customers as he might get some hasty or ignorant buyers. It may seem to some readers that this argument is a rather picayune quibble, and that this factor would never be operative to an appreciable extent in any actual market situation. However, such an objection would not be well founded, because there are a great many market situations in which this factor is an element of considerable importance.

To see this, let us consider the forces that tend to make a purely competitive market a one-price market. These forces always involve either 1. the possibility of re-contracting; or 2. the assumption that all buyers make complete surveys of the market; or 3. the assumption that all offers are known by all concerned. But, in most unorganized markets, none of these assumptions is satisfied. In most of these markets, prices are settled by bargaining, in which knowledge of alternative trading prospects is almost never complete, and varies greatly from one person to another; all offers to sell are certainly not made public in all markets, and re-contracting is seldom allowed. In markets for second-hand goods; in oriental bazaars; at country fairs; etc. these assumptions are not satisfied, and the establishment of a one-price market is a "limiting process," in the sense indicated below. In such markets as these, every time a buyer and a seller get together for trading purposes, there is a problem of bilateral monopoly, the solution of which depends on bargaining.

Conceived in this way, a market is (in disequilibrium) at any moment of time, a congeries of monopolists and monopsonists bargaining with each other. If the same group of buyers and sellers trade more or less continuously then, with the passage of time, it is reasonable to expect that knowledge of the most favorable terms for buying and selling will become more prevalent and hence buyers and sellers will begin to insist on the most favorable terms granted anywhere in the market. This will lead to a diminution in the difference between the prices charged (paid) by any seller (buyer) to any two buyers (sellers) with the passage of time and it will also lead, with the passing of time, to a diminution in the difference between the highest and lowest prices charged (paid) by any seller (buyer). This means that the prices charged for every unit will approach each other indefinitely closely with the passage of time; i.e. the prices will converge to a limit with the passage of time.[16]

If the market is purely competitive in the "Chamberlin" sense, this limit will be the equilibrium price established in a purely competitive market. Thus the usual characterization of a market as purely competitive; monopolistically competitive; oligopolistic etc. is a characterization which relates merely to the equilibrium positions which the markets approach through time. In order to describe a market completely, we need to know not only the limit toward which the dis-equilibrium prices tend, but also the speed with which they approach this limit.

Let us define as a measure of the speed of this approach, the speed with which the dispersion[17] of the prices charged in

16 The point is closely related to the remarks made in section IV of Chapter IX. What we are suggesting is one possible explanation of the actual determination of prices in a dynamic process. Alternative and far more complete explanations are developed in a forthcoming book of Tibor de Scitovzsky.

17 We may measure dispersion in any convenient way; e. g. by the variance.

the market approaches zero. If the dispersion is small, we may approximate it, in the neighborhood of the equilibrium position (where it is zero, assuming no price discrimination in equilibrium), by the first term in a Taylor expansion; this term may be designated as the rate of convergence of prices. If the dispersion is not small, the approximation may require more terms, in which case we shall have to speak of the average rate of convergence.

This convergence of prices toward an identical limit is a reasonable assumption, only if certain conditions exist in the market. For example, if all traders are in the market continuously, then price differences will very likely become known, and hence eliminated, with the passage of time. But if, on the other hand, the sellers are in the market almost continuously and the buyers come only intermittently (e.g. in oriental bazaars where travelers come, perhaps, once or twice in a lifetime to make purchases) there may not be any such tendency. If trading prices are published, as on stock exchanges, then this tendency will exist and will, ordinarily, operate with great speed. If buyers (sellers) make " shopping tours " before buying (selling), then no trading will be done except at an equilibrium price; this is the formal equivalent of the possibility of recontracting.

There is, of course, no necessary connection between this converging process and the existence of either pure competition and/or a one price market. Prices may tend toward an unique limit without the existence of pure competition; i.e. if there is duopoly or oligopoly without product differentiation (in Triffin's terminology, homogeneous competition) and the market is such that the converging process takes place. If there is product differentiation and/or price discrimination, then the prices will not converge to an unique limit, but they may, nevertheless, converge to their equilibrium values which are, of course, inter-related. In other words, we may think of the process of convergence in a single, purely competitive, market as a special case of the more general process of many prices approaching their (inter-related) equilibrium levels in a multi-market situation. However, for the sake of convenience, we may think of this latter process also as "convergence," remembering to distinguish, where necessary, between single and multi-market convergence. In the multi-market case, there may be inter-relations in the converging process which could be analyzed; but we shall not attempt such an analysis here.

The speed of convergence depends on the speed with which information is spread and the speed with which it is acted upon. At the one extreme, we have the situation where the prices approach their equilibrium levels with infinite speed, i.e. no price other than the equilibrium price can exist for even a moment. This limit is purely conceptual; the nearest approach to it in reality is to be found in organized markets such as the security and commodity exchanges. In these markets, it is the publication of prices that causes them to converge so quickly to their equilibrium levels. Ordinarily, the convergence is practically instantaneous, but this is not always true. If there are expectations of violent price changes, so that people feel that it is imperative to trade immediately, then the converging process may be delayed. Similarly any other reason that makes immediate purchases or sales essential may delay the converging process; e.g. the sudden cessation of credit for margin traders on the stock exchange. For example, on the day of a stock market crash, trading on the floor in a given security, at a given moment, may take place at markedly difference prices. In other markets, the convergence proceeds much more slowly, in the (other) limit not converging at all.

It may be that many situations which appear, superficially, to be cases of monopolistic competition, are cases where, in equilibrium, there is pure competition; but the process of convergence is so slow that we fail to recognize this fact. For example, product differentiation based on labels, packaging, misleading advertising, etc. may temporarily create price differences, which a slow spread of knowledge would, given time, eliminate; resulting in a purely competitive market.[18] However, new advertising " stunts ", etc. may continually disturb and shift the equilibrium that is being approached and thus make it appear that the equilibrium position is one of monopolistic instead of pure competition. Of course, this is merely a surmise, but it is certainly possible that it is a correct one.[19]

18 It should be noted that throughout this argument we have assumed implicitly that the equilibrium position approached was independent of the " path " of convergence. This may not always be true; for example, if the disequilibrium trades cause an appreciable re-distribution of income, the demand curve for the commodity may shift. Such cases may occur when a tourist, with a fixed budget for curios, pays excessive prices for the first few articles that he purchases and is unable to buy articles he would have purchased had he paid only the equilibrium prices for his first purchases. Or, as Professor N. S. Buchanan suggests, young couples buying furniture are often in the same circumstances.

19 In equilibrium, of course. the demand curve for the output of an individual pure competitor must be infinitely elastic.

CHAPTER XII

INSTABILITY IN A DYNAMIC SYSTEM: THE ROLE OF MONEY

THUS far, we have referred to the possibility of a dynamic system being unstable, but have not elaborated the conditions under which this situation is likely to exist. We shall now attempt to do this.

I. INSTABILITY IN A SINGLE MARKET

Usually the "laws" of supply and demand are expounded with reference to a single market which is implicitly assumed to be stable. As we have seen in Chapter IX such an assumption has implications for the structure of a dynamic system, and it is necessary to make factual assumptions in order to insure that a dynamic system (even in a single market) is stable. However, these factual assumptions are extremely plausible and it is not difficult to accept them. In fact, it is necessary to explain how it is that they might fail to correspond to the facts.

The most important source of divergence between reality and the assumptions necessary to assure dynamic stability in a single market is the existence of expectations of future prices that differ from present prices. In a dynamic system where the discounted expected future prices of X are always the same as the present price, excess demand for X is eliminated by an increase in its current price. But if expected future prices rise as the current price of X rises, this may not happen. For an increase in the expected future price of X will *cet. par.,* increase the current demand for X; i.e. there will be a tendency to substitute present for future purchases of X wherever possible.

Let us make the excess demand for X at a given moment of time, t_1, a function of (1) the excess demand for X at t_0, where t_1-t_0 is arbitrarily short; (2) the change of the current price of X between t_0 and t_1, and (3) the change of the expected future

current nor the expected future price of X changes, the excess demand for X cannot change either. At any point on OE, the ratio of the ordinate to the abscissa gives the Hicksian elasticity of expectations.[2] As drawn in figure 20, the elasticity of expectations is a constant, independent of the size of the change of the current price; Hicks' definition also assumes the elasticity of expectations to be a constant.[3] However, this need not always be the case; under certain circumstances, there are very definite reasons for supposing OE to have curvature of one kind or another.[4]

Since e_0 must have a slope of more than 45 degrees, it follows that if the elasticity of expectations is unity (when OE has a slope of 45 degrees) an increase in the current price will reduce excess demand. If the elasticity of expectations is less than one, excess demand will, a fortiori, decrease as the current price increases: (i.e. the lower the elasticity of expectations, the greater will be the tendency to delay purchases thus reducing current demand). But if the elasticity of expectations is sufficiently greater than one, it can be seen from figure 20 that a rise in price will increase instead of reduce excess demand.

We may plot the excess demand for X against time and get an excess demand time path, as in figure 11. This path could be derived from a series of diagrams, such as figure 20; each diagram showing (as figure 20) the excess demand for X at two, arbitrarily close, moments of time. If all these diagrams should reflect a situation identical with that depicted by figure

2 J. R. Hicks, "Value and Capital," pp. 205-7.

3 *Ibid.*

4 If traders in a market have a feeling that the price at t_0 is more or less normal, and the current fluctuations are merely temporary, the ratio of the percentage change in the expected future price to the percentage change in the current price will decrease with the size of the percentage change in the current price. In this case, OE will be concave from below. On the other hand, during a sharp inflation, traders may lose the feeling that the market has a norm and extrapolate current price movements. In such cases, OE will be convex from below.

20, then the excess demand time paths would move away from, instead of toward, zero; i.e. the market would be unstable.

II. Instability and Cash Balances

In the previous section we discussed the possibility of a single market becoming unstable due to the effect of expectations. Now we shall consider the manner in which the repercussions on the demand for cash balances may affect the stability of a particular market.

When there is excess demand for a particular commodity, X, (considering its market in isolation), its price will rise provided its market is stable. But an increase in the price of X may have repercussions on the demand for cash balances which will destabilize the X market. This is the more likely, the greater the proportion of the community's total expenditure that is directed toward X.

Let us consider a particular model that will illustrate this; but which also has some intrinsic interest in connection with recent business cycle theory. In this model we have two commodities; capital goods, with an appropriately weighted index number of their various prices serving as their price, and consumer goods (its price also represented by an appropriate index number). We also have cash which includes both currency and demand deposits.

We may examine this model by re-interpreting figure 20; on the horizontal axis we measure the percentage change in output of capital goods between t_0 and t_1 and on the vertical axis, the percentage change in the excess demand for cash balances occuring in the same period. (The excess demand[5] for cash balances is measured in terms of an index of both capital and

5 The concept of an excess supply (demand) of cash balances for a given individual (or group of individuals) implies the existence of a demand function for cash balances. We assume that such functions exist (for all individuals and groups with which we are concerned); and that its variables include all prices, interest rates, and incomes. For a more detailed discussion of this concept see O. Lange, "Price Flexibility and Full Employment," *op. cit.*, pp. 5-20.

will lead, via damped oscillations, to a position of stable equilibrium.

Generally, cycle theorists, in discussing such cases, conclude that a decrease in the rate of purchase of capital goods (i.e. investment) will cause a decrease in consumption which will cause a further decrease in investment and so on. Yet, these same economists would be likely to explain the shifting of resources from one industry to another, due to a change of tastes or techniques, in terms of adjustments of relative prices with but scant (if any) attention paid to monetary factors. It seems that, despite recent attempts to synthesize the theories of money and value, there is still a dichotomy between them. Economists, who are masters of both types of theory, still tend to apply either one type or the other to a given problem. And for purposes of simplicity, this may, in practical work, be desirable. However, the relationship between these types of theory should be made clear.

A simple way of doing this is to formulate a condition under which, the adjustments of a single market, or of several markets contemporaneously, can be made without creating monetary disturbances which may upset the equilibrating process. However, let us stipulate in advance that the satisfaction of this condition is neither necessary nor sufficient to guarantee that any single market or set of markets will be stable. But satisfaction of this condition will, I think, eliminate the most serious practical obstacles to the attainment of stability of the system as a whole and consequently it will prove helpful in formulating monetary policy in the later chapters.

This condition is that the *aggregate excess supply price of commodities* [9] must be equal to zero, throughout the adjustment

9 The aggregate excess supply price for commodities at a given set of outputs is the difference between the sum of the *weighted* supply prices and the sum of the *weighted* demand prices. The sum of the weighted supply (demand) prices is the aggregate supply (demand) price of the corresponding set of outputs. Both the supply and demand price of each corresponding set of outputs. Both the supply and demand prices of each commodity are weighted by the output of that commodity.

process, at the level of output[10] produced at t_0,[11] the moment at which the process of adjustment commences. When this condition is satisfied, excess supply of one product, X, will never imply an excess supply of products as a whole, but a mere change in relative preference for one as against another. A reduction in the output of X will not give rise to a reduction in the aggregate demand price for all other products, Y. In fact, it will do just the reverse; the aggregate demand price for Y will increase in order to prevent the emergence of an aggregate excess supply price for products at the previous level of output.

The continuous satisfaction of this condition through time means, in terms of our example, that every reduction in investment is compensated by an increase in consumption such that the sum of the two is, at every moment of time, the same. The excess supply price of capital goods (at the current output) leads to a contraction in their output, but the excess demand price of consumer goods leads to an expansion in their output. The adjustment in outputs and in factor allocation will then take place in the manner described in the traditional general equilibrium theory; i.e. by variations in relative prices.

It must be emphasized that this condition must be continuously satisfied in order for smooth adjustments, via relative prices, to occur. If, for example, there is a time lag between the contraction in demand for capital goods, and the expansion in the demand for consumer goods then, during this lag, the general process of contraction described above will commence. If the time lag were of the reverse kind, then a general process

10 Measured by some appropriate index number. For our purposes the exact specification of the index number is unimportant.

11 It is necessary to specify that the aggregate excess supply price is zero at the output level obtaining at t_0. Otherwise it might happen that product and factor prices decline apace, with aggregate excess supply always zero, but with a declining level of output. Such a situation would involve "monetary disturbances." In other words; when this condition is satisfied, outputs greater than (less than) that obtaining at t_0 will have a positive (negative) excess aggregate supply price.

of output expansion would occur. It must be emphasized that this condition must hold, not only in equilibrium positions, but *continuously* through time; while the system is in movement between equilibria as well as when it is in an equilibrium position.

Essentially, this condition is one form of Say's Law.[12] It is somewhat different from the condition given by Lange[13] (for the existence of Say's Law); i.e. the excess demand for cash balances is identically equal to zero. This difference can manifest itself in various ways; e.g. an excess demand for cash balances may arise from dislocations in the securities market, even though our condition regarding the commodity markets remains satisfied.

When this condition is satisfied, it becomes proper to neglect the repercussions of a reduction in the amount spent on one commodity on the aggregate demand price (for a given set of outputs) for all others. And it is this condition (or sometimes a slightly more stringent one[14]) that economists have in mind when they deal with the allocation of resources between industries. It is the obvious non-satisfaction of this condition in business cycle processes that leads them to concentrate on variations in aggregate expenditure resulting from (say) contractions in investment instead of on adjustments in relative prices.

III. Neutral Money

Many economists might agree that instability may be caused by the behavior of people with respect to cash balances, but would qualify their agreement by saying that it applies only " in the short run, but not in the long." They feel that in the " long run," the supply and demand function of each commodity,

12 *Cf.* O. Lange, " Say's Law: A Restatement," Essays in Mathematical Economics and Econometrics in Honor of Henry Schultz, edited by O. Lange, *et al.*, University of Chicago Press, 1942, pp. 49-68.

13 O. Lange, *op. cit.*

14 Namely, neutral money. On this subject see below, Section III.

factor service and security depends solely upon relative prices and not upon mere money prices. That is, they assume that if the quantity of money were multiplied by an arbitrary constant all money prices would, in the long run (given tastes, techniques and resources) increase proportionately, leaving all quantities and relative prices unchanged. When a state of affairs such as this obtains, there is said to be "neutral money."[15]

The simplest way of defining "neutral money" is: money is neutral when the excess demand for cash balances is independent (i.e. neither a substitute nor a complement) of the excess demand for any commodity, factor service or security. Thus if an excess demand for cash balances arises either because of a change in the quantity of money or in the desire to hold it, the relative prices will not change, only the money prices. Were the relative prices to change, those that changed in the same direction as the price of money (in terms of some auxiliary standard) would be substitutes with money (against the auxiliary standard) and those that moved in the opposite direction would be complements.

Obviously it would require the elapse of considerable time for the effects of a change in the excess demand function for cash balances to work themselves out so as to leave all relative prices unaffected. A change in the excess demand function for cash balances will manifest itself first in changes in expenditure on some particular articles, and will affect the prices of these articles first. These variations will then spread to other prices, and it is only after a whole process of change that all *relative* prices could return to their previous values. The variations in prices that occurred during the process obviously could not be analyzed on the assumption of neutral money. Thus the hypothesis of neutral money can, at best, be of value in studying certain problems of comparative statics; i.e. of long run equilibrium.

15 This definition of neutral money is given by O. Lange, "Say's Law: A Restatement," *op. cit.*

But there is no guarantee that money will become neutral, no matter how long an adjustment period we consider. It is one thing to postulate that all long-run equilibrium positions must have an unique set of relative prices (given tastes, techniques and resources) and quite another to prove that the various excess demand and price time paths lead to those values. Of course, it is not unreasonable to *assume* that in the long run, people do not have a " money illusion "; i.e. that their supply and demand functions include only relative (and not money) prices, and that, therefore, a position of long-period equilibrium is independent of monetary conditions. But it must be remembered that this is an assumption.

In fine, neutral money *may* be a convenient hypothesis for certain investigations in comparative statics. But it is of no use in studying economic dynamics.

CHAPTER XIII

THE THEORY OF WELFARE IN A DYNAMIC SETTING

In the preceding four chapters we have sketched the outlines of a dynamic theory and indicated some of its applications. Now let us return to the main theme of the book, welfare economics, and study it in a dynamic context.

I. Maximum Welfare in a Dynamic Context

In the first part of this book we considered the welfare properties of static systems. That is, we compared various equilibrium positions with regard to their welfare properties. But to judge the effectiveness of a set of institutions and policies in promoting economic welfare, we must consider not only how they affect the economic system in a position of equilibrium, but also how they affect it while it is in process of movement.

To do this we must introduce the concept of the *welfare-maximizing course*.[1] At any moment of time, maximizing welfare implies choosing a course for the economic system such that the present value of a stream of compensating taxes (and bounties) that could be derived from changing the course of the system would be negative—no matter what other course was adopted. If the economic system were such that any excess demand or excess price could be eliminated instantaneously, (and that in equilibrium all the maximum welfare conditions were satisfied) then following the welfare maximizing course would involve nothing more than seeing that at each moment all the conditions of static equilibrium were satisfied.

However, if only for technological reasons,[2] the economic

1 By the "course" of the economic system we mean the whole set of output, consumption and price time paths for every individual and firm in the economy.

2 For example, it requires time to adjust plants to larger or smaller outputs.

system cannot adjust itself, i.e. eliminate all excess demands and prices, instantaneously. This raises a question as to the optimum rate at which the adjustments should be made. In one sense the answer is very simple: treat products and factors at different moments of time as different factors and products and apply the inter-temporal maximum welfare conditions at each moment. Then if all firms were pure competitors they would try to combine present and future inputs, and outputs, in such a way as to satisfy the maximum welfare conditions; and so would consumers.[3]

However, in order to do this successfully, all firms and individuals must be able to make perfectly accurate forecasts of all relevant future prices. To assume they can do this is, to say the least, highly unrealistic. Thus even though the equilibrium position toward which the system was tending were welfare maximizing, the course of the system might not be. This statement is so obvious as to seem trivial, but some of its implications are of considerable interest.

Let us consider a simple one market system where, at t_0, the actual price exceeds the long-run equilibrium price. On Marshallian assumptions, this means that the supply per unit of time will increase; assume also that the change in the rate of supply per unit of time is an increasing function of the difference between the actual and the long-run equilibrium price at that moment. Consequently, the increase in supply between t_0 and t_1 will reduce the difference between the actual and long-run equilibrium price at t_1 causing a smaller increase in supply between t_1 and t_2 than between t_0 and t_1, etc., until, as t approaches infinity the increase in supply per unit of time will approach zero, asymptotically.

But such an argument presupposes that the individual firms (already in the industry, or about to enter) can correctly forecast the increased output that will result from the discrepancy

3 See above, pp. 40-46.

between actual and long-run equilibrium price. For if there were a general tendency to underestimate the increase in supply, then there would be a general tendency to overestimate the price and consequently each firm would tend to produce an output greater than that which maximizes private profit. (Assume, for the sake of simplicity that the output which maximizes private profit also maximizes welfare.) If this tendency to underestimate the increase in supply were followed by a tendency to overestimate its decrease, resulting from an

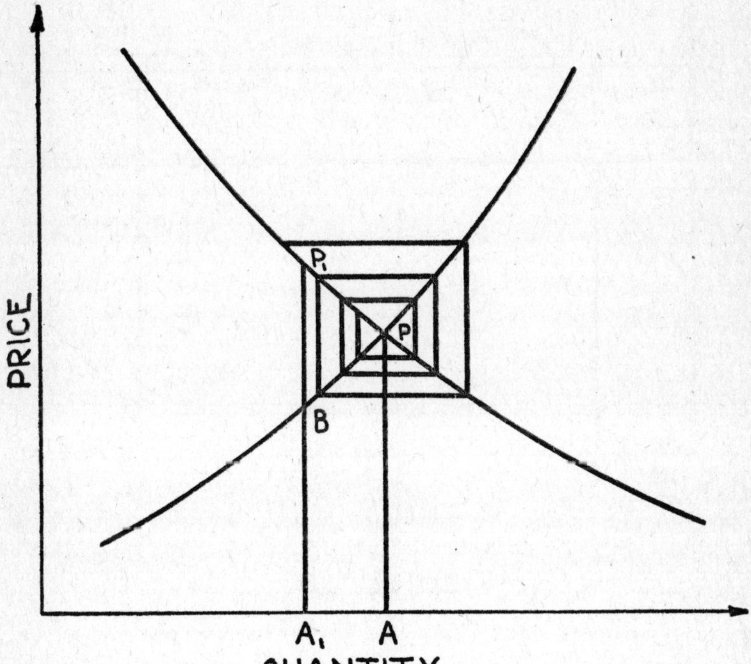

FIGURE 21

excess of long-run equilibrium over actual price, we would get fluctuations in output and price very similar to those described in the cobweb theorem.

Suppose that these fluctuations in output and price are represented in figure 21, i.e. the fluctuations converge eventually to the equilibrium position at P. Also suppose that under a cartel, the long-run equilibrium output of the industry will be P′,[4] instead of P, which it is under pure competition. If we assume that, given pure competition, welfare will be maximized in a position of long-run equilibrium, then P′, is an inferior position to P.

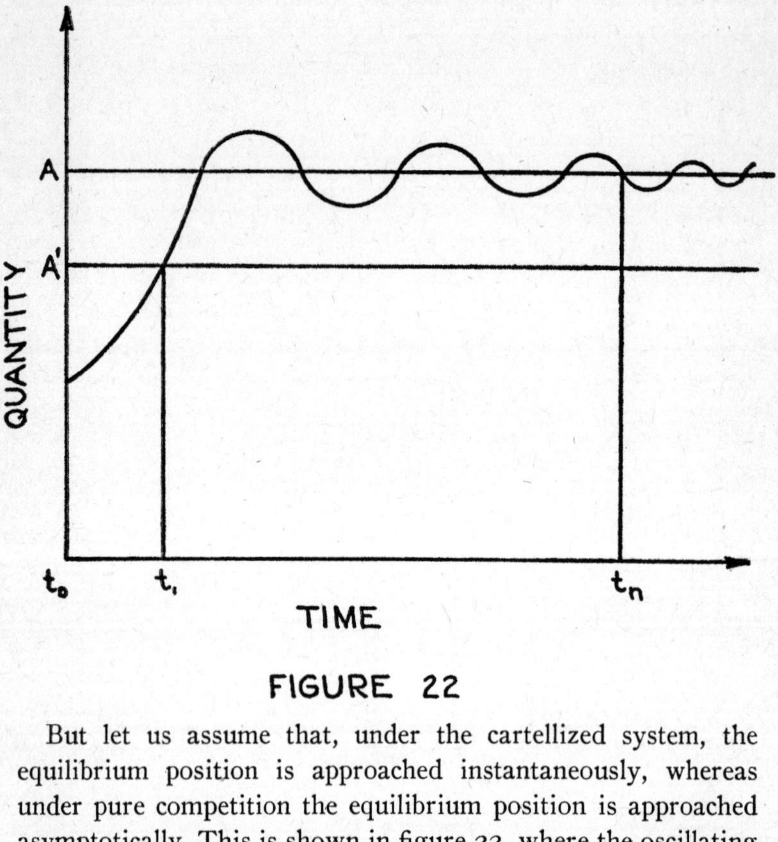

FIGURE 22

But let us assume that, under the cartellized system, the equilibrium position is approached instantaneously, whereas under pure competition the equilibrium position is approached asymptotically. This is shown in figure 22, where the oscillating curve represents the time-path of quantity under pure com-

4 The equilibrium output of the industry can be determined under these conditions if we assume 1. that the industry's demand curve is given; 2. that the cartel tries to maximize the profits of the industry as a whole and 3. that it allocates production quotas among the various firms.

petition: it approaches the equilibrium quantity, OA, in a series of damped oscillations,[5] but the quantity time-path, under the cartellized system, arrives at its equilibrium value, OA_1, instantly. We cannot determine, a priori, under these circumstances, which of the two types of organization is preferable, pure competition or a cartel. If we assume that the commodity in figure 22 is a negligible part of each consumer's budget,[6] then we may measure the welfare loss at each moment of time (by not being at OA) by the net loss in compensating taxes at that moment. For example, the welfare loss resulting from being at P_1 instead of at P, at a given moment, is the triangular area PP_1B, given our assumption that the commodity is a negligible part of each consumer's budget. The welfare gain or or loss at any moment that results from choosing a cartel (instead of pure competition) can be found by measuring the gain or loss in compensating taxes (in the above manner) that results from having the output OA_1 produced, instead of the output that would have been produced under pure competition.

5 In the usual discussion of the cobweb theorem, it is assumed that output (quantity) can change only at certain discontinuous intervals and hence the quantity time path would not consist of a continuous curve, as in figure 22, but of a series of irregular fluctuations—thus

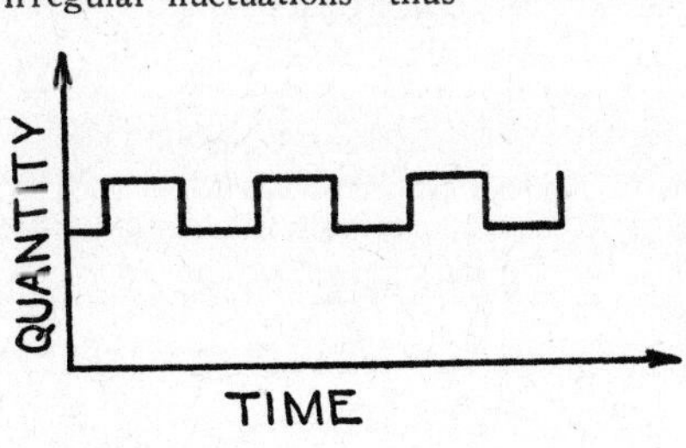

However, we do not make the above assumption, but merely postulate a tendency to "over-shoot" the mark.

6 An analogous assumption must be made for the supply curve. The assumption is that the income derived from the sale or rent of the particular factor units involved provides only a negligible portion of the income of their owners. The restrictiveness of this assumption is not of great importance for our purpose.

This assumes, of course, that the supply and demand functions remain unchanged during the period in question.

The sum of the compensating taxes and/or bounties that the state could collect, at any moment, because of the adoption of pure competition (instead of a cartel) is measured on the vertical axis of figure 23, while time is measured on the horizontal axis. The curve in figure 23 is constructed by com-

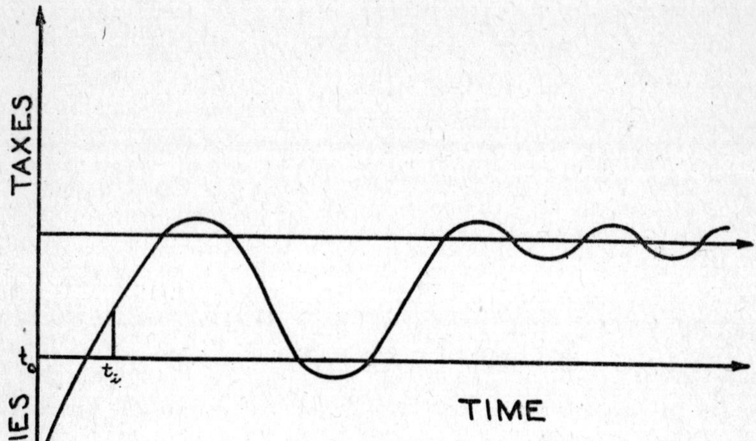

FIGURE 23

puting at each moment the compensating taxes (bounties) the state could collect (pay) because of the adoption, at t_0, of pure competition instead of a cartel. It has the oscillating shape indicated, since, in some time intervals, the quantity that would be produced by the cartel, OA_1, will more closely approximate the welfare maximizing quantity, OA, than the quantity that would be produced under pure competition. At those moments when the curve is above the time axis, the results achieved under pure competition are superior to those obtained under a cartel; and at those moments when the curve is below the time axis, the reverse is the case. The curve in figure 23 can be derived from that in figure 22 by computing the compensating taxes that could be collected (paid) at each moment because of the adoption of pure competition (instead of the cartel) provided that the demand curves of the individual consumers, for the commodity in question, are inter-temporally independent. This will be the case (approximately) for perishable commodities, e.g. fresh fruits, etc. If this inter-temporal independence does not exist, then consumers may, by judicious inter-temporal substitution, greatly diminish the welfare loss resulting from the output fluctuations assumed to occur under pure competition.

The problem of computing the compensating taxes in the general case, where demands are inter-temporally related presents no great analytical difficulty. We merely find, for each individual, at each moment, the present value of the stream of compensating taxes that could be levied were the "competitive" output to be produced instead of the "cartel" output and sum them for all individuals. To compute these taxes, we need to know the preference functions of all persons (including future as well as present commodities) and including their subjective uncertainty concerning their future real incomes and their willingness to bear it.

Our argument is, to be sure, not completely general, but generality, in this connection, is unimportant, for we aim merely to show that policies superior (on welfare grounds) in equilibrium positions, *may* be inferior during adjustment periods. We do not wish to (and could not possibly) show that they *must* be inferior.

It can be seen from figure 23 that for time periods of shorter duration than t_0 to t_1 the sum of the bounties exceeds the sum of undiscounted compensating taxes, but for longer periods the reverse is the case. Consequently, if we wish to determine at t_0, whether welfare will be greater if we adopt pure competition or a cartel, we must know the rate of interest at which the state can borrow funds.[7] If the rate of interest is sufficiently low, the present value, at t_o, of the compensating taxes, shown in figure 23 will be positive even for periods not much longer than t_i—t_o; if the interest rate is high enough the present value will be negative for much longer periods. If the state wishes to maximize welfare at t_o, it will choose that " set-up " which makes the present value, at t_o, of the anticipated compensating taxes largest. In doing this, it must determine the time interval it will consider in making its decision; i.e. it must determine its horizon. Given this time interval, if the rate of interest is sufficiently low at t_o to make the present value of the stream of anticipated taxes shown in figure 23 positive (at t_o) the state will choose pure competition; but if the rate of interest is so high as to make it negative, the state will choose a cartel.[8] In short, given the situation depicted in figure 21, it is necessary to know the rate of interest, as well as the probable interval before a new adjustment becomes desirable, in order to determine whether a cartel or pure competition is superior from the welfare point of view.

So far we have considered a system consisting of only one commodity. We may generalize our analysis, however, just as before. We may reconstruct figure 22 so that the curves represent the quantity time-path of a commodity when the effect of changes in other variables are considered. These other variables may be the quantities of other commodities, in which case, we could construct a curve in n + 1 space (one dimension for the quantity of each commodity and one for time) which would give the quantity time-path of each commodity. Problems of the sort we have just considered can be analyzed in full generality by constructing a set of such curves, one for each possible policy,

7 Although the state is a monopsonist in the capital market, insofar as loans are made for one particular purpose, we may assume the supply curve of funds is infinitely elastic.

8 This follows from the fact that the payment of a bounty under pure competition implies the payment of a compensating tax of the same size under a cartel, and conversely.

and computing (hypothetically) the compensating tax or bounty that would be paid or received under each set of conditions at each moment of time and computing the present value at t_0 of the stream of taxes and bounties paid under each set of conditions. However, there are no particularly interesting results to be found in this direction. But if the other variables are the parameters of the supply and demand curves, conclusions of some interest may be reached.

In our previous example the welfare gain made because of the superiority of the equilibrium position under pure competition to that under a cartel, may be more than offset (at sufficiently high rates of interest) by the welfare superiority of the path toward the cartel's equilibrium position. In this example, we assumed that the parameters of the system were invariant through time; that is, we derived the stream of compensating taxes and bounties (shown in figure 23) from figure 22, on the assumption that the quantity time path drawn in the latter diagram was the actual quantity time path. But this would be true only if the parameters of the supply and demand curves in figure 20 did not vary through time. If they did, the actual quantity time paths would vary also, as we have seen.

If the parameters varied only infrequently, then the actual quantity time paths would approximate, for "fairly long" intervals, the quantity time paths that would exist if the system were in a position of equilibrium that was continuously repeated. In this case, the welfare superiority of the equilibrium position attained under one type of economic organization over that attained under another, might well be the major factor in determining the desirability of the one type of organization as compared with the other. For example, let us suppose that at a given rate of interest, i_0, the present value, at t_0, of the stream of compensating taxes depicted in figure 23, will be positive if it is accumulated over a period of time not less than the interval from t_0 to t_j but will be negative if accumulated over a shorter period. So, if an interval of at least the length of $t_j—t_0$ elapses between each parametric variation, and the stream of compensating taxes that could be collected because of the adoption of (say) pure competition instead of a cartel is described by figure 23, then the welfare properties of the equilibrium *positions* will over-shadow those of the *paths toward* these positions. Under these conditions, the usual conclusions of static welfare analysis may be applied without modification.

But if the parameters were to vary more frequently than in intervals of the length $t_j—t_o$, and the situation is as depicted in figure 23, (or if the state is unable to forecast, at t_o, the situation existing after such a variation and therefore confines its " horizon " to a period shorter than $t_j—t_o$) then the welfare superiority of the equilibrium position attained under pure competition over that attained under a cartel, would be outweighed by the welfare loss sustained in the process of making adjustments. There is, of course, no presumption that the adjustment paths to positions of equilibrium under pure competition are inferior (in a welfare sense) to those toward the equilibrium positions attained under a cartel; we have assumed so merely for the sake of the argument. But, on the other hand, in the absence of perfect knowledge, or some other specific set of assumptions, there is no reason to assume the reverse.

This means that every conclusion of welfare economics (and this includes most of the major policy recommendations of economists) becomes subject to a challenge on welfare grounds. For policy recommendations have been validated by proving that if the proposed policy were adopted, the *equilibrium* position reached would satisfy the relevant maximum welfare conditions. The welfare properties of the path by which this position is reached, have never, to the author's knowledge, even been discussed. This is due mainly to a rather general tendency to regard the path leading to the equilibrium position as a " transitional " matter, which could safely be ignored. In this respect, welfare economics has been the last refuge of the

Ricardian tendency to ignore all but "long-run" phases of economic problems.

We are rather inclined to believe that many of the traditional propositions of welfare economics would emerge unscathed from a dynamic "cross-examination." But the standard "proof" of these propositions cannot be used as a basis for this belief; we must deal with the welfare properties of the paths to, and between, equilibrium positions before we can do more than take enlightened guesses as to what is the "best" policy from the welfare point of view.

It might be mentioned that many of the arguments against free trade have been based, implicitly, upon the welfare properties of the paths between equilibrium positions, while the defenders of free trade have tended to concentrate on the equilibrium positions themselves. Thus much debate on this and other issues has been beside the point, because of the failure to distinguish carefully between statics and dynamics.

The results of this generalization of welfare economics are mainly negative. A consideration of dynamic factors merely serves to make us cautious concerning the application of static welfare criteria to a dynamic world. Policies that promise to confer long-run benefits are probably sound on dynamic, as well as on static considerations; but policies that are framed with reference to transitory situations should be judged by static welfare criteria only with the greatest of hesitation.

PART III

WELFARE ECONOMICS AND FULL EMPLOYMENT

CHAPTER XIV

FULL EMPLOYMENT AND ECONOMIC WELFARE

In recent years, economists, at least in their practical work, have tended to play down the problems of resource allocation and to concentrate upon the problem of whether resources are used at all. While no one denies that it is also important that resources should be "utilized properly," there is, nonetheless, an attitude that it is one thing to get the resources employed and another to get them into their optimum uses.

It is, I think, also correct to say that there is a widespread feeling, although it is by no means unanimous, that it is more important to get resources, particularly labor, immediately employed in doing something, than to proceed more deliberately in the hope that they will eventually find more useful occupations.

In this and the following chapter, we shall analyze the welfare implications of these beliefs.

I. Employment and Welfare in a Simplified System

Let us begin our analysis by studying a drastically simplified economic system; the relevant complications will be brought in at a later stage of the analysis. Assume that 1. our analysis is confined to a definite period of time, t_1—t_0, during which all factor prices are constant; 2. that at the set of factor prices current during t_1—t_0, there will be a positive aggregate excess supply price, defined as above (p. 150), for product output at the quantity that would employ all factor units willing to work at the going rates of reward; and 3. that there is, for relevant range of output,[1] an infinitely elastic supply[2] of every

1 The "relevant" range of outputs for any product is the range between the output at t_0 and the output that would be produced at t_1 if at t_1 there were "full employment." "Full Employment" exists (in this model) when

product with respect to its own price (after *all* repercussions, occurring in t_1—t_0 are taken into account; i.e. an infinite *total* elasticity of supply) during t_1—t_0, at the prices current during this period. Given factor prices (by assumption 1) assumption 3 implies that if the demand curve for X should shift to the right (due to an increase in the money income of the community) the price of X could rise (if at all), for only a very short period of time (less than t_1—t_0), because as soon as it did, supply would increase until it was brought back to its previous level.

Under these conditions, the unemployment existing between t_0 and t_1 is simply a result of a failure of the community to spend sufficient money for the purchase of products. The unemployment represents a loss of output to the community, for if some persons were (say) given presents of cash, assumption 3 implies that the resulting increase in their expenditures would increase output and employment. It can be shown that this loss of output represents a welfare loss to the community, First, assumptions 1 and 3 together imply that the owners of the idle factor units (particularly labor) would be willing to let them out for hire at the going rates of reward, or very likely for less, and thus the increase in expenditure will increase the welfare of the owners of the factor units that would otherwise be idle. Furthermore, assumption 3 implies that when there is less than full employment, extra quantities of product upon which newly created money is spent would be forthcoming without an increase in price and thus no one's real income would be reduced by an increase in the quantity of money, while some persons (those who receive the presents and (probably) the owners of the factor units that would otherwise

---

there is a zero aggregate excess supply price for commodity output at the level that would employ all factor units willing to work at the going rates of reward.

2 Since we are *not* assuming that every product is produced under conditions of pure competition, this assumption implies a certain type of price policy.

be idle) would have theirs increased. Therefore, increasing the real output of the community, under these conditions, would increase welfare and consequently creating the extra money necessary to accomplish this result is defensible on welfare grounds.

In short, given these assumptions, a policy of achieving full employment cannot cause any welfare loss (*during* t_1—t_0) from the misdirection of resources, which would have to be set off against the welfare gains derived from achieving a fuller utilization of them. But if we consider a longer period of time than t_1—t_0, such losses may, as we shall see, occur. In addition, the assumptions made imply that so long as there is less than full employment, increased expenditure will not cause any prices to rise (during t_1—t_0); this greatly simplifies the problems of Monetary and Fiscal Policy.

II. Full Employment and Monetary Policy

In the light of the preceding arguments it would seem, therefore, that a policy of maximizing welfare would lead the authorities to increase expenditure. The question is how to accomplish this. Many methods of achieving this result have been suggested, but the most simple, and analytically most interesting is that suggested by Prof. A. P. Lerner.[3] He suggests that we simply print the money in appropriate quantities and distribute it in such a way as to induce a rate of expenditure sufficiently great to achieve full employment.

Lerner's proposal may seem very shocking, and at first blush, it would appear that there must be something wrong with it. However, given the assumptions of our model, Lerner's position is unassailable. On our assumptions, increasing the quantity of money (assuming that an increased quantity of cash will lead to an increased rate of expenditure on products) simply increases expenditure on products (without affecting their prices) and hence increases their output, which increases real income

3 A. P. Lerner, "Economics of Control," *op. cit.*, Chapter XXIV; "Functional Finance and the Federal Debt," Social Research, February 1943.

and, as we have seen, welfare. But our assumption 2., specifies that there is less than full employment. What if there should be full employment?

A full employment situation, in terms of our simplified model, would be one where assumption 2. would read: " At the set of prices current during t_1—t_0, there would be either a zero or negative aggregate excess supply price for product output at the quantity that would employ all factor units willing to work at going rates of reward "; and where assumption 3 would read: " there is a zero elasticity of supply of every product (with respect to its own price after taking into account all repercussions occurring from t_0 to t_1) at the outputs current during t_1—t_0, i.e. at full employment; " assumption 1. would remain unchanged. In such a situation increasing the quantity of money could only raise the product price level; it could not affect real income, except to redistribute it.

Therefore, on our assumptions, monetary policy becomes a fairly simple matter. Merely determine whether or not there is full employment; if there isn't, then increase the quantity of money by having the Treasury make presents to suitable persons (i.e. persons who will spend the gifts—the relatively poor) until the positive aggregate excess supply price for products at the " full employment " output is eliminated. Once full employment is achieved, it is necessary only to decide upon a desired product price level. Then, if there would be a negative aggregate excess supply price at that price level, simply reduce the quantity of money until the aggregate excess supply price (at that price level) would be reduced to zero.

In short, when there is less than full employment, the government must pay out more than it receives (printing the difference) so as to increase aggregate expenditure on products; when the product price level is higher, at full employment,[4] than some desired level, the government must collect more than it

4 Assumptions 1 and 3 preclude the possibility of the price level rising at less than full employment.

pays out (sterilizing or destroying the difference); at full employment and the desired price level, government receipts would equal disbursements, thus balancing the budget.

At this point, the reader is likely to begin to chafe under our assumptions. But we must ask him to remain patient a bit longer. For we wish to show that borrowing instead of printing the money introduces no fundamental change into our analysis. It is important to do this because economists, who advocate policies such as the above, usually shy at the idea of printing the money, and instead speak of borrowing it.

That is, when there is less than full employment they would have the government issue securities which it would exchange for cash. If the securities were bought by commerical banks who created new demand deposits in the process of making the purchase, then money will have been indirectly created. If, however, they are purchased by investors (including institutions), then the government has acquired cash balances from persons who would not have used them to purchase products [5] and transferred them in one way or another to persons who will; i.e. the government has increased the income velocity of circulation rather than the quantity, of money.

If, at full employment, there is a negative excess supply price of commodities at the desired price level, then the government must collect a budgetary surplus. However, it should not use the surplus funds to reduce the outstanding National Debt; this should be done only when the government wishes to increase the quantity of money in circulation; i.e. when there is less than full employment. Using a *previously acquired* [6] Treasury surplus to reduce the national debt when

5 If the bond purchasers would otherwise have spent the funds on products, or have loaned them to persons who would have, then the bond sales will not increase aggregate expenditure on commodities.

6 It is essential to emphasize that the surplus was previously acquired. A surplus currently being acquired is highly deflationary and will certainly inhibit any attempt to foster increased expenditure on commodities. However, this has nothing to do with a previously acquired surplus.

there is less than full employment will simply transfer cash from the Treasury to the erstwhile bondholders. Insofar as the bondholders consider commodities better substitutes for cash than for securities, this will increase expenditure on commodities. But in practice, bondholders, particularly institutions, are not likely to have their expenditure patterns greatly affected by Treasury action of this kind. Thus reducing the National Debt is not likely to be an effective method of increasing employment.

If the surpluses collected in periods when the government is trying to keep the price level from rising happened to offset the net borrowings in periods of less than full employment, there would be no secular tendency for the national debt (held outside the Treasury) to rise. If the surpluses exceeded the borrowings, the debt would tend to fall secularly and if the converse were true, it would have a secular tendency to rise.

This raises the question as to what would happen if the debt should continually grow larger. The question of how the debt burden can best be distributed raises practical problems of public finance which are quite involved and with which we can not concern ourselves here.[7] However, it is necessary that we indicate the significance, or lack of it, of the Public Debt from the welfare point of view.

From the welfare viewpoint, the Public Debt can create only distributive problems. It consists, after all, of mere paper claims and while the satisfaction of these claims may very well alter the distribution of wealth and income this is of no consequence for welfare (as we have defined it). For it is always hypothetically possible to re-arrange the system of taxation so as to distribute wealth and income in any manner desired. In practice, of course, with a given system of taxation, the distributive effects of a large debt may be quite serious, but that is another problem.

7 For an excellent theoretical discussion of this question see E. D. Domar, "The 'Burden of the Debt' and the National Income," *American Economic Review*, Dec. 1944, pp. 798-827.

But it might be argued that a large Public Debt would affect welfare adversely on account of the effect heavy taxation might have on the desire to work; bear risks; etc. To make such an argument valid requires two assumptions: 1. that there is full employment and 2. that the response of individuals to a reduction in the marginal reward (after taxes) of effort or risk-bearing is to reduce the amount of effort or risk-bearing that will be forthcoming in the relevant situation.

In the absence of full employment there is no a priori reason why a large Public Debt must create a large tax burden. For, given our assumptions, the interest on the Debt could be paid (in the absence of full employment) by printing money, and the result would be merely to increase employment and welfare. If there were full employment (or if the printing of sufficient money to service the debt would bring the system to full employment and in addition create an upward pressure on the price level) then an increase in the size of the Public Debt would imply an increase in the tax bill.

An increase in the tax bill (assume that the only tax levied is a progressive income tax) will affect the desire of individuals to work; bear risks; etc. via two channels: the "substitution effect" and the "income effect." The substitution effect [8] refers to the fact that a variation in the rate of reward for working would cause an individual to vary the amount of work he would perform per period of time (e.g. per week) even though he were given a compensating tax or bounty such that after he had made his optimal adjustment he would be on the same indifference curve as before. The income effect refers to the effect of the compensating tax (or bounty with a reversed sign [9]) on the number of hours of labor he would perform per period of time.

8 The terms "income effect" and "substitution effect" are defined in a manner similar to that in which they are defined in the "theory of consumer's choice," *cf.* J. R. Hicks, "Value and Capital," pp. 29-33.

9 This is because we are defining the income effect (on the number of hours worked) as the difference between the actual change in hours worked

The substitution effect of an increase in an individual's tax bill (when the tax is a progressive income tax) is to reduce the net reward he receives per hour of work and thus (assuming his indifference curves are convex to the origin) to reduce the number of hours per week that he will work. The income effect of such an increase is more difficult to determine and it is probably the more important: it might very well be that individuals are so anxious to preserve a given level of disposable income that a reduction in gross income will simply make him work [10] more. On the other hand, if a very large fraction of income increments (decrements) must be paid (deducted) as taxes, an individual may feel that "he might as well take it easy." However, in either case, the effect of the tax will be to reduce welfare.

The welfare loss caused by a tax can most easily be be understood by considering that almost all taxes violate one (or more) of the marginal conditions of maximum welfare.[11] For example, an excise tax violates the fifth marginal condition;[12] an income tax violates the sixth and seventh marginal conditions etc.[13] In fact the only practicable tax which would not violate any of these conditions is a simple flat personal tax that is absolutely independent of anything that the individual owns or does. For such a tax would not affect the *marginal* cost of buying, selling or making anything or the *marginal* reward of per-

---

and the change that would have taken place had there been a compensating tax (bounty) levied. This is not quite analogous with Hicks' definition, but the difference is unimportant for our purpose.

10 Our discussion has run in terms of the incentive to work. However, there would be no difficulty in adapting it to a discussion of the incentive to bear risks, or to save. On this subject *cf.* W. S. Vickrey, *Agenda for Progressive Taxation*, Ronald Press, 1947, p. 336; also Appendix VI.

11 *Cf.*, p. 18.

12 *Ibid.*

13 *Ibid.*

forming any service, and would thus not prevent the satisfaction of any of the marginal conditions. However, such a tax would be independent of ability to pay and would thus be repugnant to current notions of fiscal justice. In addition, it would probably be impossible to raise very large revenues if the amount of taxes that could be collected from each individual were restricted to the amount that could be collected from the poorest. Thus for societies with large budgets, a tax system which does not violate some of the criteria of maximum welfare is a chimera. In short there is no simple way of predicting the effect of an increased tax burden on the willingness of the members of a society to work; bear risks; etc. But it is clear that a heavy tax burden may create real problems from the welfare point of view. It is therefore important to consider the possibility of an interest-free Public Debt, but such an investigation would take us very far afield.

III. Unemployment and Welfare: A Further Consideration

Let us now consider a bit further the relationship of unemployment to welfare. We stated above (p. 182) that the owners of idle factor units, particularly labor, might be willing to accept a smaller money reward than that currently offered and thus be able to pay compensating taxes if jobs could be found or created at the current rate of remuneration. But this immediately raises the question of why these factor units do not underbid the current rate and secure the existing jobs for themselves; this is the old question of whether there can be involuntary unemployment at positive wage rates.

However, if we consider the problem in a dynamic context, it becomes apparent that even if we were to grant that involuntary unemployment is incompatible with long-period equilibrium, there would still be a time interval (during which real and money wage rates would be adjusting themselves to their equilibrium levels) within which workers would be idle even though they were willing to accept both lower money and real wage rates than those currently offered.[14] During such an adjustment period, many workers might be willing to accept lower wage rates than those currently offered, but would not yet have made this willingness effectively known.

Considered in a less "mechanical" way, an unemployed person might well be willing to take a lower wage than that currently offered at any given moment, provided everyone else doing similar work would also accept it. But he is rather reluctant to accept less than others are getting for similar work; it is a blow to his self-esteem. In other words, the utility functions of these workers include, as variables, the earnings of other persons doing similar work. They will be less satisfied, given their own incomes, if other persons doing similar work receive more than they do, than if they received the same reward or less.[15] Consequently, although they might not be willing to work for less than the wages currently received by those employed, if they were given jobs at current wage rates a compensating tax (perhaps sizeable) could be levied upon them.

Another factor to consider is the lack of perfect foresight. To accept a position (at less than the current rate of renumeration) involves diminishing (if not altogether eliminating) that possibility of getting another job opportunity, perhaps at the current rate. And the temptation is to hold out a little longer in the hope of getting such a job. It is only as the period of unemployment lengthens and hope beings to fade that the "asking price" of the unemployed begins to fall below the wage paid those who are employed.

While this is by no means an exhaustive explanation of the

14 *Cf.* the present author's article "Interest and Employment," *Journal of Political Economy*, June 1946, pp. 243-57.

15 *Cf.* above, pp. 64-7.

" wage psychology " of the unemployed, it should be sufficient for our purpose; namely, to explain how it is that unemployed persons may be unwilling to work for less than the current rate of reward and yet be more than willing (i.e. capable of bearing a compensating tax) to accept a position at the going wage rate.

IV. Some Reflections on Waste and Welfare

It may have seemed strange to the reader that in the preceding discussion of public spending, no attempt was made to specify how the money was to be spent. However, if the argument of this chapter is granted, it is a matter of no importance. We showed, in the first section of this chapter, that (given our assumptions) welfare will be increased by printing money and giving it away. This means that welfare will be increased by such a procedure so long as the work, if any, performed by the recipients is not an actual public nuisance.

Of course, if the recipients of the money are compelled to perform tasks whose value to the community[16] exceeds the value of their foregone leisure by more than the amount given (either as a gift or as a reward for performing the work), then welfare will be greater if the recipients perform such work. However, if the state is constrained, by political considerations, from putting resources to work in their most " welfare increasing " occupations, then welfare *might* be greater if the state did not put anyone to work as an adjunct of its money creating activities, but instead simply created and distributed enough money to achieve full employment. The state would probably have to create more money to achieve full employment if the money is given away, than if it is used as a reward for work, because in hiring people, the government reduces the number of jobs that must be provided by private industry in order to achieve full employment. But since the marginal cost of creating

16 Measured by the algebraic sum of the compensating taxes and bounties that could be collected and paid on account of it.

money (i.e. of creating the physical means of payment is zero, during t_1—t_0), or practically so, this should not be considered.

From the welfare point of view, the decision as to whether to give the money away or to make the recipients work for it depends upon whether welfare will be greater if the government hires the otherwise unemployed factor units directly or if it merely creates sufficient effective demand to induce private industry to employ them. In other words, if the government were employing (say) 2,000,000 men (and printing the money to pay them) would welfare be increased if the government were to discharge them and create (and distribute) enough additional money to induce private industry to hire them (because of the resulting increased demand for commodities)? [17] The answer to this question, of course, depends upon how the government (and private industry) would use these resources.

It may seem peculiar that we should be able to increase welfare by "currency juggling," or by "hole-filling" etc. But the peculiarity lies in the assumptions we have made about the economic system. A properly functioning economic system economizes its resources so as to get the utmost from them; to increase the output of one commodity necessarily implies a reduction in the output of something else—or in leisure. But if some of the resources are to be involuntarily idle, then the situation is quite different. For then, we may have more of whatever these resources can produce without giving up anything—except unwanted leisure.

The waste of resources lies not in their being used to construct relatively unnecessary public buildings—or even in "hole-filling"—but in their not being used otherwise. Government spending involves a waste of resources only insofar as the resources would have been put to better use by either the

17 The reader might well object "if you distribute largesse in this manner, you will destroy the incentive to work." Insofar as this is true—and it might very well be true—it is an important, perhaps crucial, factor and must be taken into account.

government or private business. If the resources would otherwise have been idle, their utilization for *any* purpose not a public nuisance, is productive, i.e. not wasteful.

Arguments of this kind have sometimes been termed "upside down" economics. And that is a very appropriate name for them. For when there are unemployed resources, the economic system is, in a sense, inverted. It is not productive resources that are scarce and to be economized; it is opportunities to use them that are treasured. We do not create goods and services; we create jobs, and the goods and services which flow from employment are more or less incidental. Insofar as resources are idle, the things they can produce are akin to "free goods" and *any* scheme to capture them becomes "sound economy."

Some readers might object that we have been dealing with a caricature of a government spending program. They would argue that a dollar of government spending is as productive (measured by the algebraic sum of the compensating taxes and bounties, the payment and collection of which it makes possible) as a dollar of expenditure by private business. Insofar as this is true, it implies that even if there were full employment there would be an insufficiency of government rendered services (as compared with the welfare maximizing amounts) and that hence welfare could be increased by levying appropriate taxes and spending the proceeds to render these services.

It must be noted that such an argument is an argument for more government spending even at full employment and not merely an argument for "making work." The welfare basis for this type of argument is simply the usual one that a particular use of funds by the government justifies the taxes levied in order to secure them.

It might very well be true that more expenditure by the government (and the levying of the necessary taxes) would be justified even though there were full employment. However, many economists question this hypothesis and our argument has been, and will be, mainly concerned with those cases that emerge on the assumption that it is not true. (Any argument for government spending that is valid when there is full employment is, a fortiori, valid when there is less than full employment.) It is theoretically important to examine such cases, for it is in connection with them that new ground can be broken in the theory of welfare economics.

CHAPTER XV

STUMBLING BLOCKS ON THE ROAD TO FULL EMPLOYMENT

IN the simplified model that we constructed in the last chapter, welfare would always be increased by increasing employment. Furthermore, increasing employment and output, when there was less than full employment, could not lead to any price increases and thus the authorities could pursue full employment single-mindedly, without worry of inflation. It was important to examine carefully the properties of such a model, since it is only in such a model that the pursuit of full employment does not entail any untoward consequences (i.e. mis-allocation of resources or inflationary tendencies); and it is there that we can clearly envisage the full force of the arguments for "full employment" policies. But now let us consider some stumbling blocks that must be circumvented if we are to attain both full employment and a satisfactory, if not an optimum, allocation of resources.

I. INFLATION WITH UNEMPLOYED RESOURCES

In the simplified model discussed in the preceding chapter, the monetary authorities might be confronted either with the problem of eliminating unemployment or that of combating inflation, but never with the problem of doing both simultaneously. Our assumptions removed the possibility of both problems arising simultaneously. If they cannot arise simultaneously, monetary and fiscal policy is tremendously simplified. If there is unemployment, the treasury should acquire deficits; if there is inflation it should acquire surpluses. But, if there should be both unemployment and inflation, the treasury is faced with a difficult problem of deciding which of the two it is more anxious to combat.

If we relax either assumption 1 or assumption 3, or both

together (while retaining assumption 2), it becomes possible to have both unemployment and a rising price level. Let us consider first a rather simple case; suppose that trade-unions, aware of the government's full employment policy, decide to force a given increase in money wage rates per period of time. Let us also suppose, for the sake of simplicity that the increase is to be proportional for all wage rates. Then, assuming a static technology, it would follow that all other factor prices, and product prices as well, would rise. (Whether or not they would rise in the same proportion as money wage rates is not important, for our purpose.) And this may happen while there is still an appreciable amount of unemployment. If it does, the government will be forced to choose between maintaining the current level of product prices and raising the level of employment. If it taxes vigorously (piling up a budgetary surplus) to prevent the price level from rising, the higher money wage rates will reduce employment. If it does not, the price-level will rise.

Nor can the government count on the opposition of employers to higher money wage rates to hold them down, if it is adopting a full employment policy. For then the employers can simply "jack-up" product prices in proportion (or more than in proportion) with the increase in wage rates, without fearing a loss of markets; the government will have to create the effective demand in order to provide full employment.

But the trade unions are not necessarily the only, or even the chief, villain of the piece. Once markets are guaranteed them by a full employment policy, oligopolists may lose all sense of proportion and make tacit agreements to raise prices to almost any level. In practice, it is likely that both the unions and oligopolists will be a constant source of inflationary difficulty under a policy of full employment. To some extent the tendency of prices to rise may be offset by the constant lowering of unit costs due to technical progress. But there is no guarantee that the inflationary pressure on the commodity price-level from the trade unions and business will just offset the deflationary pressure of technical progress. In short, a policy of attaining full employment is by no means enough to determine an adequate fiscal and monetary policy. Such a policy must be carefully integrated with a wage and price policy; unless the income share of the fixed income groups is wholly a matter of indifference. Perhaps, a partial solution would be to make all contracts in terms of a "wage-unit," thus avoiding many of the untoward effects of a constant increase in the price level. But we cannot go into details on such matters.

If we drop assumption 3 (which is quite unrealistic), we may take into account the rather obvious fact that any attempt to increase the general level of output will almost certainly bring about an increase in prices. That is, to approach full employment, starting from a position of less than full employment, inevitably involves, to some extent, the raising of the price-level, and the changing of relative prices. The practical questions for the monetary authorities are always by how much is the price level to be allowed to rise; how fast is it to rise; and what changes in relative prices are to be permitted.

It would be intellectually very satisfying to apply our welfare criterion to determine how much of an increase in the price level should be tolerated for the sake of reducing unemployment by a given amount. Unfortunately, however, the criterion is not altogether satisfactory when applied in this context. Nonetheless, let us apply it, and save our doubts until later.

If the three assumptions listed on p. 181 were satisfied, and if all factor unit owners (particularly laborers) were willing to let their factor units work for less than the current rate of reward, then welfare would be increased by increasing employment. Insofar as an inflation merely redistributes income in an undesirable way, it would appear that welfare (viewed ex post and assuming compensation to be paid) would always be increased (so long as we confined ourselves to t_1—t_0) by increasing employment. If we considered a longer period, there might ensue a mis-allocation of resources that would have to be considered. On this see section II of this chapter.

However, in practice, compensation will not be given to those damaged by a rise in the price level. And consequently, since fear of the ravages of a rising price-level is very widespread, it might well be that, viewed ex ante, a prospective increase in employment (and real income) accompanied by a rise in the price level would decrease welfare. Thus an increase in employment may affect welfare, viewed ex ante, quite differently than welfare viewed ex post. It is for this reason that we feel that our welfare criterion (ex post) is not altogether satisfactory as a *sole* criterion for determining policy in such matters. But nonetheless, the ex post welfare criterion does serve to indicate one important factor in the situation which should not be neglected.

II. Unemployment and Resource Allocation

In this section we propose to show how an attempt to attain full employment during t_1—t_0 may have adverse effects on the allocation of resources and may thus be incompatible with a policy of attaining maximum welfare. So long as we deal with a model defined by the three assumptions made in the preceding chapter there can be no possibility of an increase in employment causing a misallocation of resources; for all factor units are virtually immobile as between industries [1] and the only problem is whether or not they are to be employed in the industry to which they are attached. Thus so long as we confine our purview to t_1—t_0 there is no need for concern as to the effect of an increase of employment on the allocation of resources. But if we consider a longer period of time, problems of this kind may arise.

For example, it may very well be that the attainment of maximum welfare would require that the labor force attached to some industries contract, in order that the force attached to

1 We use the term "industry" here in its loose, broad connotation; e.g. as in the Census of Manufactures, rather than in the more narrow sense in which it is used in economic theory.

others may expand. However, if the government provides jobs for everyone either at his current occupation (or at some occupation akin to it) or at some "make-work" [2] government job at the current wage rate, then the incentive for the workers to shift occupations will be materially lessened, if not altogether destroyed.

But, it may be asked, won't variations in relative earnings in the various occupations accomplish the reallocation of resources? To this, two answers may be given. One is that relative wage variations may accomplish the reallocation but much more slowly than if there were the additional goad of being unemployed if one is attached to the "wrong" industry. In fact, without unemployment as a spur to change occupations, the occupational redistribution of the labor force would be accomplished mainly via the entrance of new workers into the labor market; i.e. very slowly.

A second answer is that in an economy where trade unions are important, the effectiveness of relative earnings as a guide to the allocation of the labor force is very questionable. If the workers attached to one particular industry find that they are earning less than those attached to another, they are very likely to attribute it to the greater success in bargaining by the union in the other industry and demand that their own leaders get them increases. Thus relative earnings may have little or no power to reallocate the labor force between industries.

This suggests that, from the welfare point of view, there may be losses from an inferior allocation of resources to weigh against the gains to be derived from continuous full employment. In order to maximize welfare at t_0, we must compare (as in Chapter XII) the time paths of the compensating taxes and bounties that follow from adopting each of many possible policies, and adopt the one which makes the present value, at t_0, of the algebraic sum of the compensating taxes and bounties

2 A job where the value of the product is considered as secondary—if at all.

with correlative labor shortages elsewhere in the economy. Thus monetary and fiscal policy should not, from the welfare point of view, be determined solely with an eye to the number of unemployed.

When there is a very large amount of unemployment, it is likely that aggregate expenditure on commodities will be too small and the recommended fiscal policy will incur a deficit just as an ordinary full employment policy. So long as the level of aggregate expenditure on commodities is too small, the policy we are recommending—call it a "Modified Full Employment Policy"—is identical with an "ordinary" full employment policy. But once it reaches this level, it does not propose to make jobs, but to re-adapt the labor force to fill the jobs that already exist.

If tastes and techniques were unchanged, following such a policy would eventually lead to full employment. But it would not, at t_0, aim to achieve employment at t_1 or any other date. And, since tastes and techniques are constantly changing, full employment would probably never be actually attained. There would always be a certain number of persons (perhaps sizeable) in process of transfer from one industry to another; the number depending on the number and kinds of changes in tastes and techniques to which the economic system is subjected.

III. Some Objections to a Modified Full Employment Policy

There are at least two difficulties with our Modified Full Employment Policy that are likely to strike the critical reader at once. Let us discuss these in order:

1. THE COST OF OCCUPATIONAL TRANSFER

A reader with a strong feeling for humanitarian considerations may object to leaving perhaps millions of persons unemployed until they change their occupation. Given the plight of the unemployed individual under present institutional arrangements such an objection carries considerable weight. In fact, if we hark back to Chapter VIII, we shall be reminded of the strong possibility that on an ex ante basis, welfare may be decreased by pursuing policies that increase welfare ex post, because of the undesired risk of uncompensated individual loss.

As our society is at present organized, everyone is compelled, willy-nilly, to become an entrepreneur—an entrepreneur in his own talents. Preparing oneself for an occupation involves undertaking an investment which can fare badly for reasons quite apart from individual merit; e.g. change in tastes and techniques. And if the investment turns out to have been unwise, the result is likely to be a ruined career and perhaps a wasted life. It is no wonder that there should be a demand for guaranteeing people jobs in their own occupations.

However, there is really no need to do this in order to grant the individual security. What we would suggest is that persons attached to industries or occupations that are overcrowded, be offered opportunities to re-train themselves for fields in need of additional personnel. At government expense, they would be paid the current reward of their current occupation while re-training. Thus unemployment would not involve any personal loss to the unemployed or diminution in expenditure on products.

Those who wished to stay at their old occupation would, of course, be free to do so, but they would have to accept the consequences. If more than the optimum number chose to leave an occupation, the government's re-training subsidy would be given mainly to the younger workers, since the investment in their talents would be more productive than in the case of older workers. Conversely, workers too old to re-train advantageously could be subsidized to stay at their jobs.

Such a scheme as this would obviate much of the fear of unemployment without destroying the mobility of the labor force or wasting its power in performing tasks less productive than it is able.

2. OBSTACLES TO TRANSFER

Many readers are likely to complain that our worrying over the improper allocation of resources due to the pursuit of an "unmodified" full employment policy is rather naive. After all, with restrictions on the mobility of resources being what they are, there is no a priori reason to suppose that freezing people at their present occupations by giving them jobs, will greatly worsen the allocation of resources. Insofar as this is true, and (in my opinion) there is a great deal of truth in it, it greatly reduces any conceivable welfare advantages of the "Modified Full Employment" policy over the unmodified version.

However, an economic policy bent on attaining as high a level of economic welfare as possible, must not only pursue full employment, but must also smash all restrictions on the mobility of resources. Our proposed re-training program will eliminate some of the restrictions; i.e. lack of capital to facilitate mobility. But it is also necessary to compel some trade unions to change their entrance requirements; to compel monopolists and oligopolists to remove restrictions on entry into their fields and to engage in genuine price competition.

CHAPTER XVI

CONCLUSION: A PHILOSOPHIC REFLECTION ON WASTE AND WELFARE

ACTUALLY, most advocates of full employment policies would probably swallow our proposed modification without difficulty, and could probably show that they have always advocated similar "modifications." However, they might argue that it would be no small matter to remove existing institutional restrictions on the mobility of resources. And that, failing this, it would still be desirable to eliminate unemployment, irrespective of resource allocation.

Their argument might take two forms. One is that the danger of welfare loss from additional resource mis-allocation caused by public expenditure is unimportant as compared with the loss from unemployment. With this judgment, I should be inclined to agree, but it must be emphasized that it is a matter of judgment. Confidence in this judgment will be strengthened if we consider welfare from the ex ante point of view.

The other argument would not be a welfare argument at all; it would be rather an argument on "socio-political" grounds. Unemployment involves more than a mere economic loss; it robs the individual of his initiative and his self-respect. In his resentment and frustration, he becomes fertile soil for all sorts of doctrines subversive of free institutions. Our social order depends upon the immediate elimination of unemployment whenever and wherever it appears, and this objective has priority over all others.

Broadly speaking, one of the advantages of our great wealth is that we can afford to waste. As we become increasingly rich, it becomes increasingly unnecessary to scrimp in order to get the very utmost from our resources. Even if we were to grant (which we do not) that guaranteeing every individual a job in his current occupation were subversive of welfare, viewed ex post, we would still argue that we are rich enough to bear the loss in the name of social peace and good order.

INDEX

Date Due

HOPE COLLEGE LIBRARY
B171 .R4 R 101010 00H
Reder, Melvin Warren,
Studies in the theory of welfa
0 1127 0093636 5